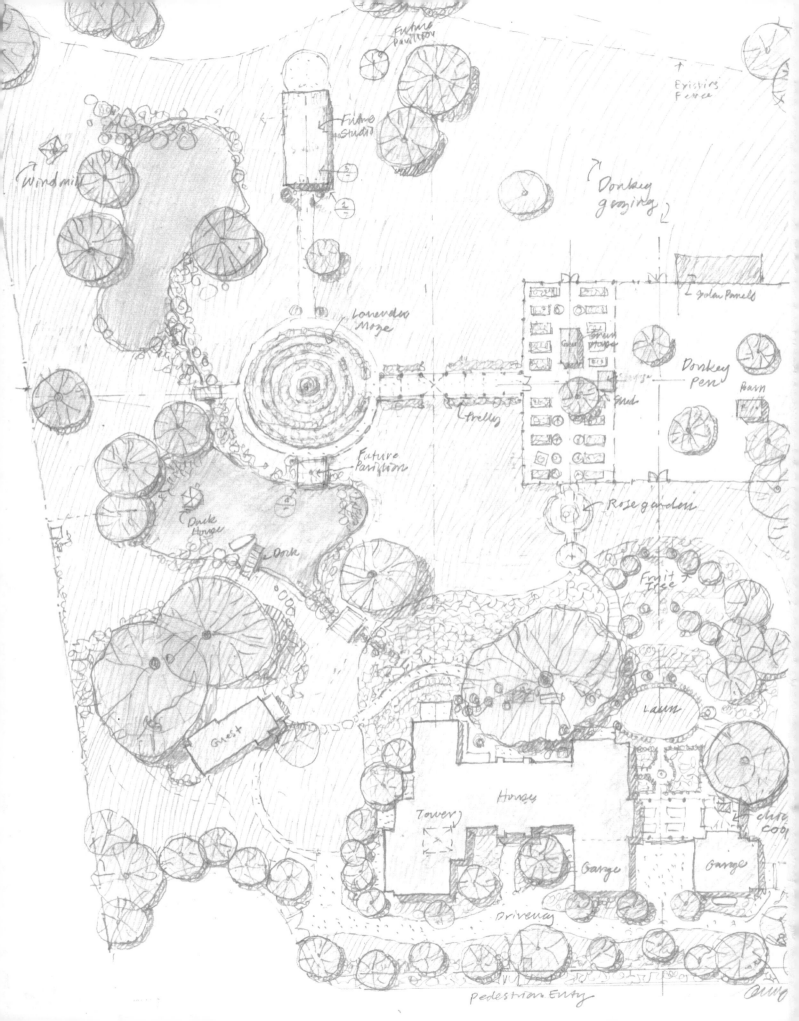

Windmill

Future
Pavilion

Future
Studio

Existing
Fence

Donkey
grazing

Lavender
Maze

solar Panels

Donkey
Pen

Barn

Trellis

Future
Pavilion

Duck
House

Dock

Rose garden

Fruit
Tree

Guest

Lawn

House

Tower

chicken
coop

Garage

Garage

Driveway

Pedestrian Entry

Patina Farm

Patina Farm

Brooke Giannetti and Steve Giannetti

To our children,
Charlie, Nick and Leila,
for giving our dreams meaning.

Foreword

There are a lot of properties in the world that make a statement. Some are brash, some bold, while others are simply brilliant. The Biltmore in North Carolina is best known for its sheer size as the largest house in America. Hearst Castle in San Simeon can be counted on for its grandiosity and opulence. And think about Monticello for the brilliance of its design, much of it cutting-edge in the late eighteenth century. But, of course, a house doesn't have to be big to make an impact. Cole Porter's legendary pied-à-terre at the Waldorf Towers was a master class on chic style in the 1950s, and Vogue editor Diana Vreeland's apartment, which was ablaze in red chintz—her "garden in hell," as she put it—was as much a reflection of her as the clothes she wore. As with Vreeland's home, the common thread with all of these places, big or small, is that they encapsulated their owners' visions, personalities and desires in exacting detail and with a confidence not often seen in design today.

But, right now, on five acres in the heart of the Ojai Valley in California, is a place that has emerged over the past three years as the best case study of confident design married with passion and purpose. It's not as over-the-top or attention-seeking as some of the aforementioned homes. In fact, it excels in its understatement. Hidden from street view by a bank of white roses, the house and landscape—treated as one—fosters a respect for nature, for space, for light and air. There, everyday moments are celebrated, and that place is Patina Farm.

The vision that Brooke and Steve Giannetti have executed celebrates the good life and the art of living well. Artfully designed and executed, the house—like its owners—is a study in unpretentious elegance. Casual, comfortable style blurs the lines between indoors and out. Yet beyond the stalwart stone façade, hand-finished plaster walls and antique tile roof, it's the spirit of the place that emanates. When you're at Patina Farm, you feel it through the waft of lavender in the backyard, the sound of crunching pea gravel underfoot on the back terrace, boughs of freshly cut lemons on the kitchen island, the jolly nature of miniature donkeys and Silkie Bantam chickens that have the run of the place.

And while the owners didn't set out to create a Biltmore or Monticello (and why would they?), there are, indeed, similarities: a demand for authentic materials, an unerring eye for quality craftsmanship, a respect for nature and, it goes without saying, the reverence for a beautiful patina, whether it be from the timeworn finish on an antique Swedish table, a tarnished silver box or a thread-bare French bergère. The Giannettis' quest for the best, as well as living consciously—right now, in the moment—is a testament to their passion for life, which has a lasting impact greater than any brick and mortar structure. That's the story and legacy of Patina Farm.

—Clinton Smith, Editor-in-Chief, *Veranda*

Introduction

For Steve and me, our dream to build Patina Farm started as a few small seeds of change. We had enjoyed living in our lovely home on a small lot in Santa Monica for 10 years. A seed that began as a few vegetables in some planters blossomed into a large kitchen garden where our front lawn had once stood. Another seed grew into a chicken coop large enough for eight hens to roam.

The focus of our free time began to center on nature. I spent more time tending to the garden and the chickens, Steve found calm painting landscapes, and our daughter Leila discovered a love for horses. The happiness and satisfaction of these new experiences furthered our desire to make larger changes to our life—to think of a life beyond our small suburban lot, a life on a farm.

During this same time, opportunities were guiding us towards our new life. A design project in Ojai introduced us to an idyllic country town surrounded by natural beauty, where we discovered a lush five-acre piece of land with plenty of room for gardens, assorted animals and an artist's studio. As we started to realize that our seedling ideas were now blossoming into a beautiful dream, we spent all of our free time imagining Patina Farm.

We began the process using the same design philosophy that we described in our first book, *Patina Style*, finding inspiration in the natural beauty on the property that would eventually surround our new home. The colors in the landscape helped us refine our palette and finish selections. They would include natural materials that would age beautifully over time—galvanized steel, chalky limestone, and pale white oak. Our selections would include antique elements that would bring their own history to Patina Farm—grayed vintage barn beams as well as faded antique wood doors and moss-covered terra-cotta roof tiles from

The design of Patina Farm mixes classical and modern architectural details. In our entry hall, an elegant series of vaults appear as if they were sculpted out of white plaster. Having no baseboard or moldings around the doors or on the ceiling gives the space a more modern aesthetic.

When we first drove up to the property, we fell in love with these two magnificent oak trees. We knew that they would become the centerpiece of the design of our new home.

France. These worn elements would be balanced by the modern simplicity of smooth white plaster walls, clean sheets of glass and slender steel doors. Bringing these pieces together would produce an interplay between rustic and refined.

As we continued our search for inspiration, Steve and I also reminisced about our past experiences and family history. During these discussions, it became obvious that the design of Patina Farm would be influenced by Steve's classical architectural training as well as his time spent in his family's ornamental plaster studio. The materials, textures and colors of Giannetti's Studio provided some of the strongest inspiration for Patina Farm. The chalky palette of vintage plaster and wood carvings combined with scaffolding shelves, galvanized metal and aged concrete, all covered with a fine layer of white dust, created the perfect palette. The casual display of the items stacked on the floor and shelves is reflected in the way we used decorative plaster pieces in our home.

As our dreams came to the fore, the design of our home began to unfold and we started to look for elements that we both loved. I found myself drawn to the Belgian design aesthetic to which I was first introduced in Belgian Pearls, the blog of my friend and talented interior designer Greet Lefèvre, who generously shares the best of Belgian design. I immediately gravitated toward the designers who combined ancient and modern elements. So we decided to

take a trip to Belgium, where we visited Greet and other designers. We also carved out a few days to visit Paris, where we found inspiration for Patina Farm in the architecture—the building materials, colors and scale of the buildings. And then there were the flea markets. We were in heaven at the Marché aux Puces, exploring the beautifully displayed booths, visually absorbing the patina of vintage copper pots, chalky galvanized bins and tattered leather books. Deep stacks of antique paneled doors leaning casually against the walls of one stall called to us. We examined them all, imagining where we could use them in our new home, and selected a set of graceful paneled doors that would be perfect for the wall behind the desk in my office.

The artifacts that we purchased in Belgium and France would solidify the look and feel of our home. They would inform all of the design decisions and selections in the coming months.

During our various journeys, Steve drew in his sketchbook, documenting particular building features that inspired us. As we gathered inspiration, we found Pinterest to be an indispensable organizational tool. We created online boards that enabled us to file images by category, and I added comments to many of the images to remind myself of the specific detail I liked in the photograph. I also edited our boards as the design process progressed, deleting photos that were no longer relevant.

Before making any decision about the floor plan for our house, we focused on the physical location of the house on the property. The position of several majestic oak trees was particularly impactful. We staked the house on the site and envisioned the views that our windows would frame. We watched the sun rise and fall on the lot and were inspired by the perfect pink moment—the incredible sunset for which Ojai is famous.

We considered various influences during this phase. The most important were sunlight; topography, including the location of large trees; views from different locations; proximity of neighbors and their animals; and, of course, the numerous city and county rules and restrictions.

For us, sunlight is priority number one. We are always aware that the direction of the sun and how it arcs across the property greatly affects the light quality inside the house as well as the nature of light in the outdoor rooms that we create. Ideally the longest facade of the house

The classical architecture and industrial building materials that are mixed
on the shelves of Giannetti's Studio provided some of the strongest inspiration for Patina Farm.
It is these unique pieces that fill Patina Farm with our personal history.

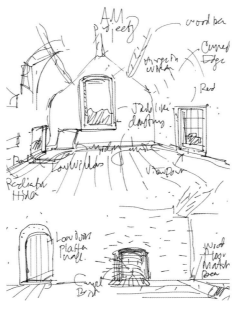

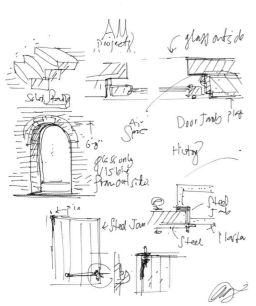

should face south. We were fortunate to be able to situate our house so that the back elevation faces south, allowing us to flood the main public spaces and the outdoor seating areas with the most desirable light during the day. We also wanted to let light in through two or three sides of every room, to balance the light in the rooms and allow light into the spaces for a longer part of the day.

During this part of the design, we also focused on the unique characteristics of the site. The five acres we purchased had its challenges: approximately one acre was at street level; the rest of the land was much lower. There were also a couple of very large oak trees to take into consideration. While these characteristics put constraints on our location options, they could also enhance the design of the house, depending on where we decided to place it. The oaks, for example, limited the usable square footage, since legally we were not allowed to build in the drip line of the trees. However, if we could figure out how to design the house to fit between the city setbacks as well as beyond the drip line, the trees would provide much-needed shade for the majority of the house as well as add a gorgeous backdrop.

Ultimately, we decided to site the house on the higher level of our land; but before we made the final decision, we played a game of "what if": What if we put the house on the lower portion of land? The mountain view would be better and the house could have a large yard adjacent to it, but the longer run for the driveway and utilities would add greatly to the cost. We would also miss out on living in the shade of the magnificent oak trees. It was settled. The higher part of the site was right for us.

We decided to create an H-shaped plan with two main courtyards. The southern court in the rear of the house sits entirely in the shade of a 250-year-old oak tree, perfect for cooling the area in the summer months and letting the warming rays of the sun come into the house in the winter. The northern courtyard provides an arrival area and allows for a lovely garden area between the driveway and the front door.

We hope you enjoy touring Patina Farm in the following pages. We are delighted to welcome you into our home.

Steve's paintings, sketches and photographs helped document details that we would eventually use at Patina Farm. We collected antique doors and architectural elements to infuse our new home with European history.

Arriving

We thought about Patina Farm as a series of experiences. After all, that is what we were really creating—places for things to happen, emotions to be felt, and memories to be made. Our vision of Patina Farm was of a place where we would live with family, friends and animals that was peaceful, relaxed and beautiful. Every design decision we made, from the selection of plant material to the location of every room would need to support our vision. We wanted people to feel the serene emotional tone before arriving. You catch a glimpse of the bell tower through the sycamore trees as you drive down our street; a profusion of white roses covers the front fence, letting you know that you are at the right place. You hear the gentle splash of water and as you peak through the roses to see a rustic fountain fashioned from a galvanized equestrian tub and a tarnished spout.

As you enter the gate, the animals will greet you. Thelma, Louise and Dot, our diminutive African Pygmy goats, position their necks for some gentle rubbing, as Daisy and Buttercup, our miniature Sicilian donkeys, nibble the grass under the limbs of the sycamores that border the gravel drive. The presence of the animals adds to the "country path" air of the meandering driveway.

The color palette for Patina Farm begins in the front garden with gentle soft gray wood, white and blush-colored roses, silvery French lavender and westringea, and the natural varied greens of the sycamore trees and native grasses.

Like some of our favorite houses, we wanted Patina Farm to feel as if it had been built over time. The "original" main portion of the house has plaster walls and an antique tile roof that reflect the Spanish colonial heritage of Ojai, while the rustic wings of the house, with their weathered gray cedar walls and galvanized metal roofs, recall barn structures from the neighboring farms and might have been added at a later time. With a desire to limit

The glass and steel doors allow our visitors to see through the house from the front door to the gardens beyond. The creamy French limestone flooring on the exterior front landing and the interior entry hall makes a seamless transition from outside to indoors.

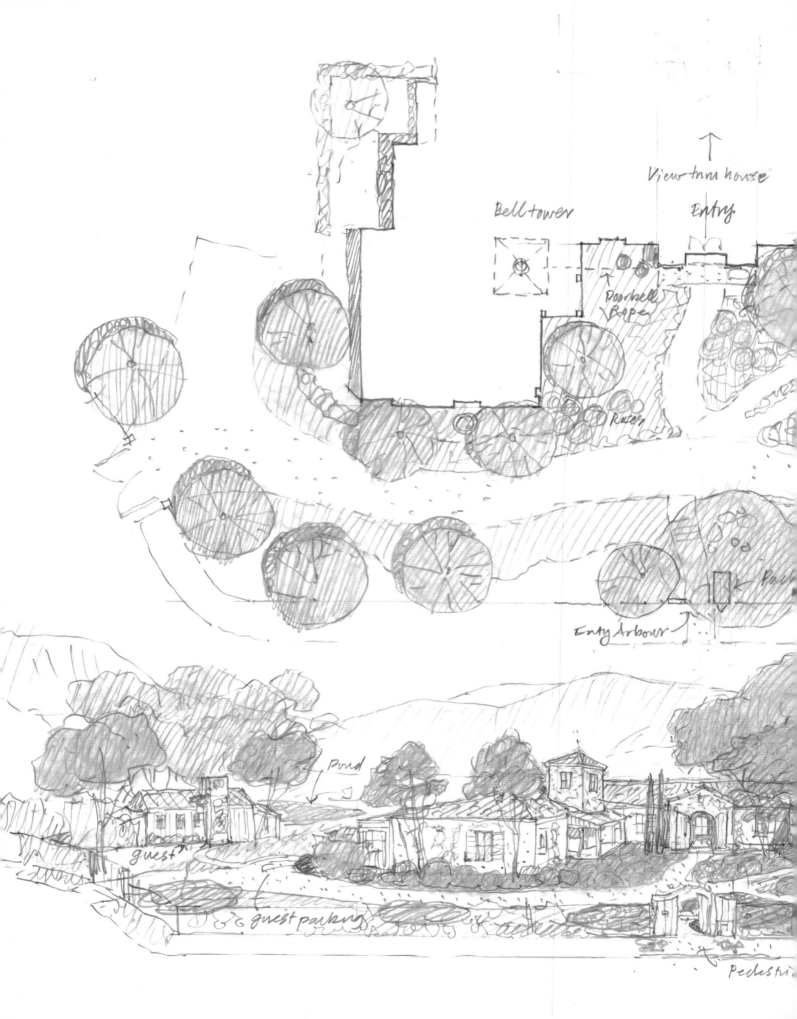

View thru house

Bell tower

Entry

Doorbell
Rope

Roses

Entry Arbour

Pond

guest

guest parking

Pedestri

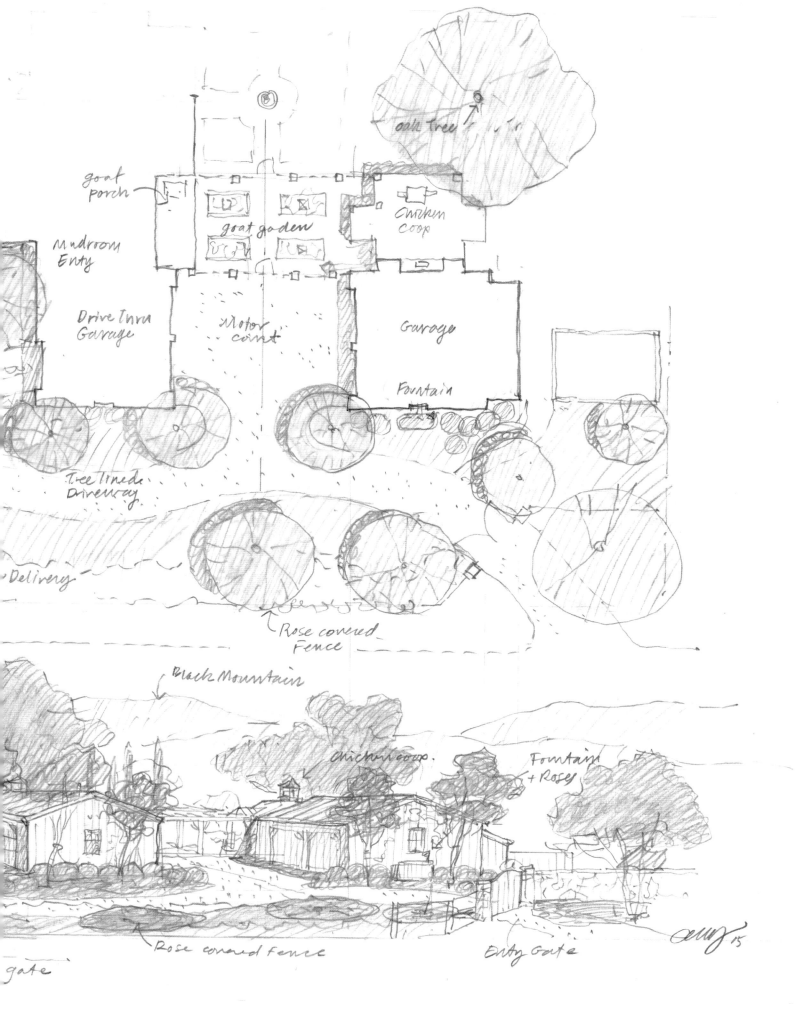

oak Tree

goat
porch

Mudroom
Entry

goat garden

Chicken
Coop

Drive Thru
Garage

Motor
court

Garage

Fountain

Tree Lined
Driveway

Delivery

Rose covered
Fence

Black Mountain

Chicken coop

Fountain
+ Roses

Rose covered fence

Entry Gate

gate

The oversized blooms of our Polka rose vines are beautifully balanced with the muted silver and green foliage in our gardens. During the spring, these vibrant roses frame the entry gate. Next to the front door, an antique wooden urn mold suspended from a pulley connects to the bell in the tower. Visitors young and old can't seem to resist ringing the bell.

our materials palette and connect the different parts of the house, we constructed all of the shutters on the main house from the same gray-stained cedar boards. Stone veneer washed with soft linen grout covers the entry, tower and fireplace, creating the third, and oldest layer of our story.

The front door, made of steel and glass, invites your eye into the house as well as providing an opportunity to catch sight of the expansive vista beyond. This initial experience reveals the connection of the indoor and outdoor spaces that flows through the entire house. The front door is flanked by large operable shutters, which we close against the west sun in the late summer. On the shutters, a rope and pulley system connects to an antique schoolhouse bell in the tower that guests can ring to let us know of their arrival.

The front garden is a balance for formal and informal. "Little ollies" (a bush related to the olive tree) shaped into spheres mix with natural flows of lavender and white roses. A combination of catmint and lamb's ear grows in the middle of the gravel driveway, giving it the feel of a country lane. A glimpse of the goat garden can be viewed when the doors on both sides of the garage are open.

Starting at the front gate, we wanted to create an emotional response with our design of Patina Farm. The sound of splashing water and the sight of our rose-covered "barn" garage creates a serene atmosphere for our visitors as they begin their journey down our gravel drive. The limited palette continues a feeling of calm through all of the gardens.

Connecting

The primary goal of all of the spaces we designed at Patina Farm is to increase our connections with the individuals that we love. This includes the bonds with our friends and family as well as our relationship with our animals.

We made several design decisions with this objective in mind. Our choice of an open floor plan was one key to allowing our entire family to be together, even if we aren't necessarily sharing the same task.

The fluidity of the floor plan also makes the spaces more malleable; for instance, the dining room can alternatively be used as a meeting area or homework space. The family room, with its large seating area and ample window seat, is the perfect place for large gatherings or for a quick nap in the sun.

Since there are few walls separating the spaces, the light quality is also maximized. The slender 3/4-inch steel door and window mullions increase the amount of glass, allowing unobstructed sunlight to flood the space from the many windows and doors on the north and south walls. The underlying philosophy for our lighting is to illuminate the walls and ceilings and create a warm reflected glow. In the evening, as natural light dims, we rely on chandeliers, wall sconces and table lamps to create an overall glow rather than the harsh light that canned lighting in the ceiling would provide. To that end, we use picture lights to light wall surfaces and artwork, be it a collection of plaster ornaments from Giannetti's Studio or travel sketches. Small chandeliers illuminate the vaulted entry hall ceiling, painting the surfaces with a warm light.

We committed to the same natural color palette that we used outside for all the home's interiors, reinforcing the fluidity among the indoor spaces as well as the connection among the indoor and outdoor spaces. The walls are covered in Diamond Kote by Western Blended—a thin layer of plaster over drywall, to mimic the stucco walls outside. This surface reflects the light beautifully, creating a luminous depth. French limestone flooring connects the interior and exterior spaces and complements the color tones in the stone walls. Three panels of Gracie hand-painted wallpaper

PREVIOUS OVERLEAF: *Rather than dedicating a separate room just for formal dining, we placed our dining table in the center of our home, where it can easily be used for meetings and school projects as well as casual meals. Sitting between the two pairs of glass doors makes it feel like we are eating outside in the garden.*

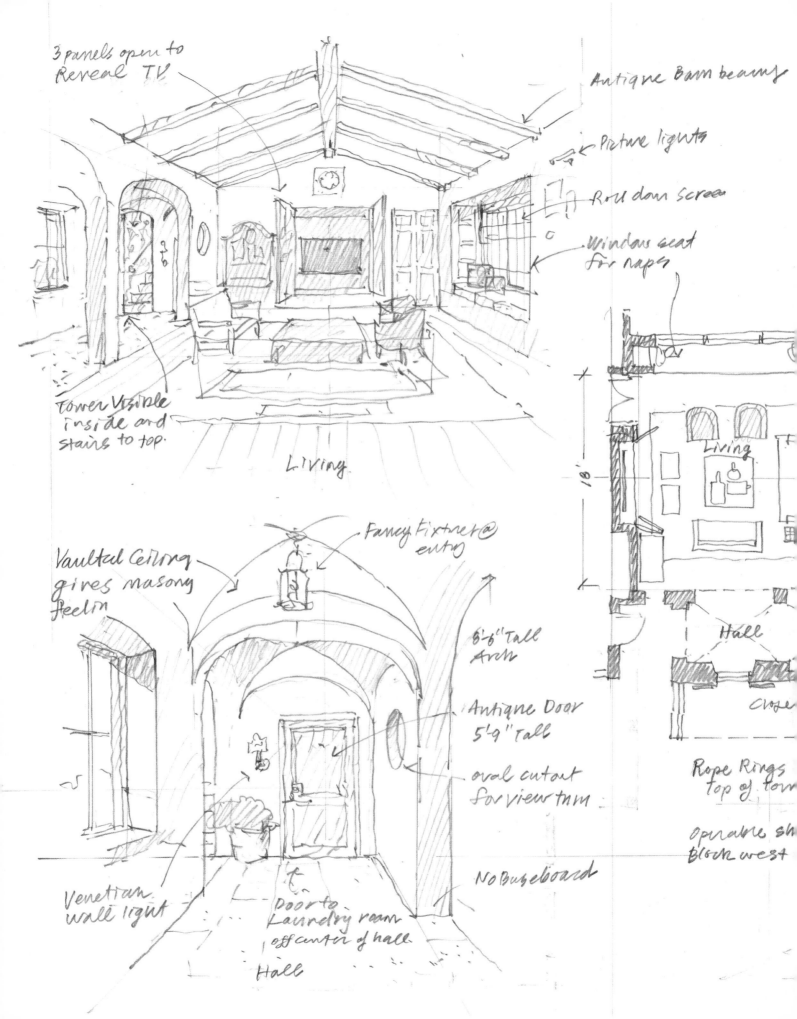

3 panels open to
Reveal TV

Antique Barn beams

Picture lights

Roll down screen

Window seat
for naps

Tower visible
inside and
stairs to top.

Living

18'

Living

Hall

Vaulted Ceiling
gives masonry
feeling

Fancy Fixture @
entry

8'-6" Tall
Arch

Antique Door
5'-9" Tall

oval cutout
for view thru

No Baseboard

Closet

Rope Rings
top of tower

operable sh-
Block west

Venetian
wall light

Door to
Laundry room
off center of hall

Hall

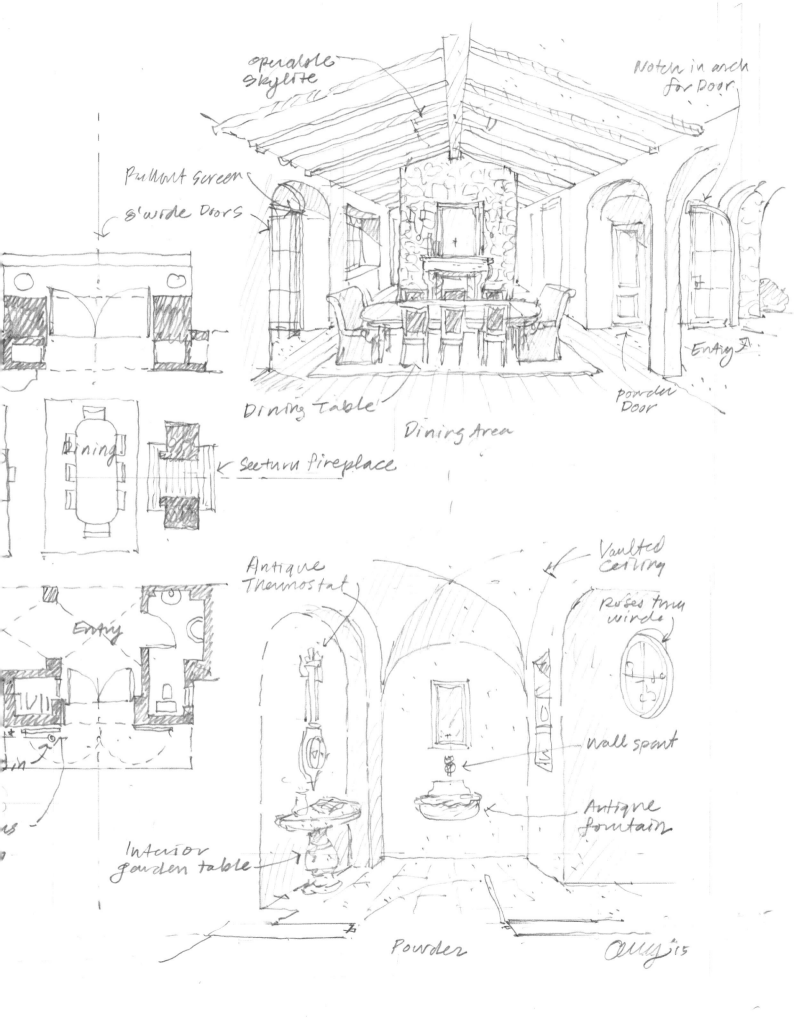

operable
skylite

Notch in arch
for Door

Pullout Screen

8' wide Doors

Entry

powder
Door

Dining Table

Dining Area

Dining

See-turu Fireplace

Vaulted
Ceiling

Antique
Thermostat

Roses thru
windo

Entry

Wall spout

Antique
fountain

Interior
garden table

Powder

OPPOSITE: *The stone wall of our tower and the placement of garden elements inside the glassed-in walkway create a visual connection to the outdoors.*

unify the color scheme while doing double duty as a beautiful focal point for the main room and television camouflage. The wood panels are installed with pivot hinges on each end and a large piano hinge on the center door. The cabinet inside is lined with plain Gracie paper the color of the background of the panels, providing an attractive, deep blue backdrop for the television. (We prefer televisions mounted lower when possible, as this is a far easier position for watching.)

We chose relaxed, natural materials that would forgive the heavy use they would encounter in our home, filled with children and pets. Sofas and ottomans covered in washable neutral linens and well-used vintage leather chairs invite visitors to relax, put up their feet, and stay a while. Our material selections add to the calm, informal atmosphere. The clean plaster walls ensure that the warmth of the vintage barn beams and the paneled French pine doors, as well as the detailed limestone quatrefoil, feel neither fussy nor dated. Our whitewashed European oak floors only look better as their finish mellows over time. Durable vintage wool rugs in taupe, aqua and cream define the spaces.

The flowers and foliage from outside find their way into every room of the house in the form of informal bouquets, potted topiaries and a large tree in the family room. Screen doors that pocket into the wall, as well as retractable window screens, allow us to enjoy fresh air even when the summer flies are at their peak.

Our desire was to combine both modern and classical architecture in our home, like we had seen in many of the European homes that inspired us. We showcased antique doors as art pieces, hung on pristine white walls. We built a vaulted entry made sculptural without the fuss of moldings or trim. A small notch detail in the arched ceiling allows us to open the front doors 90 degrees while still allowing us to continue the arches throughout the space. The entry, with its lower ceilings, also provides a more intimate welcoming space for our guests.

With the desire to use all of the space the house offers, we designed storage in the thickness of the plaster walls.

The flush plaster-covered doors of the coat closet by the entry and the two storage closets on either side of the back doors make these much-used repositories virtually invisible. Plaster shelves for displaying family photos are carved into the walls on both sides of the window seat.

In addition to housing the front door bell, the upper part of the tower is a small library accessed by a very steep ladder-type stair made from scaffolding boards. I lined the stairs with a collection of old leather books in a haphazard "Hogwarts" display. We find quirky items like the too-steep stair and the too-short door to be important to making a house charming and unique.

Placing this antique door in a clean plaster wall, allows the craftsmanship of the original door hardware to be appreciated. The door is only 69 inches tall. The small scale provides an illusion of sorts, making the space appear longer than in reality.

We filled the rooms at Patina Farm with antique pieces that we love. Swedish antiques tend to have perfect proportions and just the right amount of detailing. Because we are always filling vases with freshly cut flowers from the garden, we chose to plant flowers that would complement the interiors of Patina Farm.

*The jewel box of a powder room, with its combination of rustic and refined as well as indoor/
outdoor pieces, quickly tells the story of the entire house. A marble sink from Belgium is
suspended on the wall, with a fountain spout repurposed as a faucet. All of the pipes are hidden
and can be accessed from the kitchen pantry, which is behind the sink wall. A detailed
eighteenth-century gilt barometer is paired with a rustic stone demilune next to the sink.*

Nourishing

As with the other rooms at Patina Farm, the kitchen was designed with our family and friends in mind. The main living space flows easily into the kitchen, separated only by the two-sided stone hearth that warms both spaces. The inspiration for our kitchen was the rustic European farmhouse kitchen. The center island works well for shared cooking as well as for serving meals family style. Stools provide comfortable seating for friends to chat while the meal is being prepared.

The kitchen is also connected to the rest of the house via materials and color palette. The same white oak was used to build the cabinetry and center island as well as the panels that cover the refrigerator. The outdoor limestone became the backsplash for the range as well as the hearth. Natural linen found on the upholstered pieces is also used as panels under the sink and in the pantry.

The unobstructed view through the windows above the sink links the kitchen with the outdoors while providing sweeping light into the space. Below the stone quatrefoil that we purchased in Belgium, is a Lacanche range, the formidable focal point of the kitchen, where copper, aged brass and stainless steel mix beautifully.

We used antique pieces, like a painted French cabinet, in place of new cabinetry wherever possible. Our pretty white dishes are stored in open display, but the toaster oven, microwave and coffee maker are stored behind cabinet doors near the sink, hidden but easily accessible. The pantry is tucked behind the antique cabinet. Keeping appliances off of the counters and storing dry goods out of the way contributes to the uncluttered calm.

Although the center island appears to offer just seating and open shelf storage, it affords a wealth of hidden storage. The side of the island facing the stove is equipped with drawers, which are filled with baking utensils and spices. Cabinet doors conceal deep storage for oversized pots and baking trays as well as a trash bin.

During the design process, we were always thinking about ways to connect the interior rooms with the gardens. Having the large steel windows go all the way to the countertop and building storage shelves into the side plaster walls gives an unobstructed view of the gardens from the kitchen.

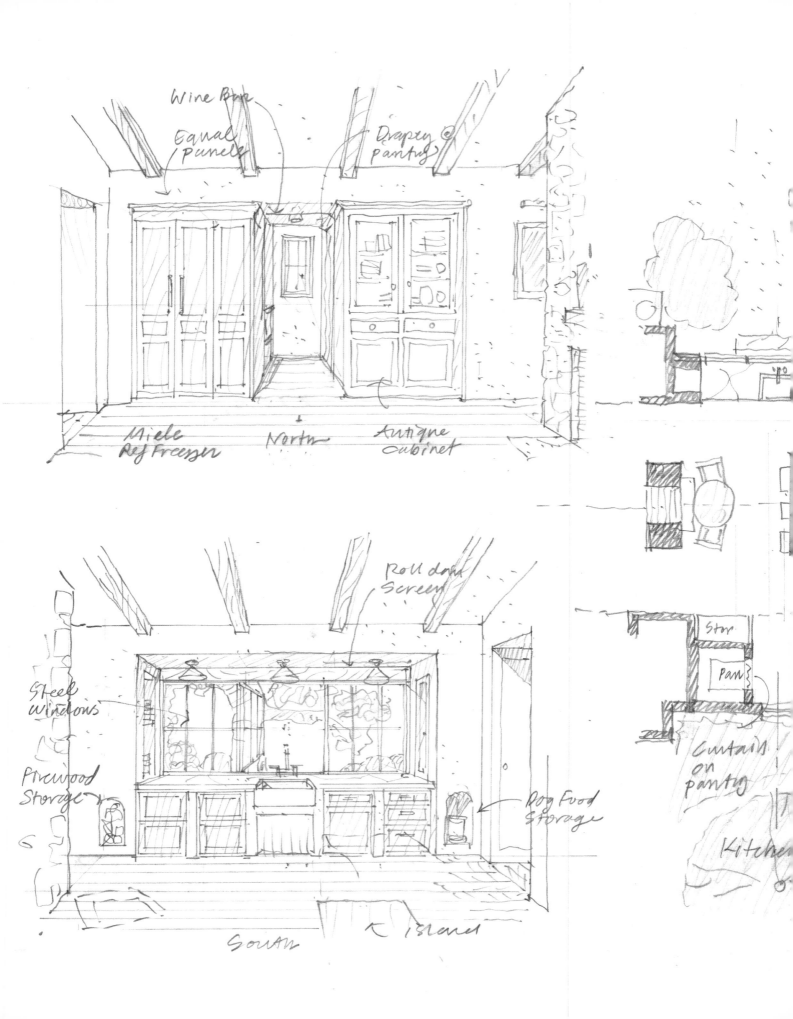

Wine Bar

Equal Panels

Drapery @ pantry)

Miele Refreezer   North   Antique Cabinet

Roll down Screen

Steel Windows

Firewood Storage

Dog Food Storage

South   ← Island

Stor

Pan

Curtain on pantry

Kitchen

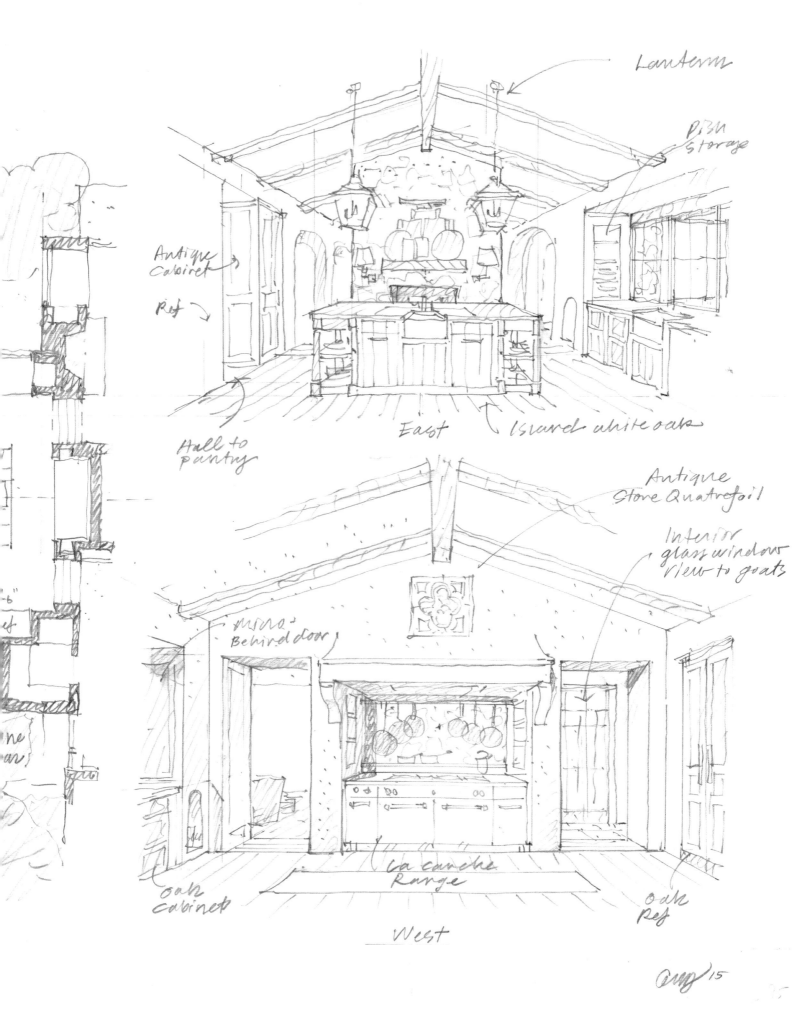

Lantern

Dish
Storage

Antique
Cabinet

Ref

Hall to
pantry

East   Island white oak

Antique
Stone Quatrefoil

Interior
glass window
view to goats

Mirror
Behind door

La canche
Range

oak
cabinet

oak
Ref

West

amy 15

We embrace the beauty of natural materials. Copper, brass and stainless steel mix wonderfully in our kitchen. Our pots and pans hang above the range, making them easily accessible for everyday use. Utensils, stored in a white earthenware pitcher are also close at hand. OPPOSITE: I prefer a single-bowl kitchen sink to a double bowl. Our large 30-inch farmhouse sink works well for washing large pots and pans.

A continental-height table paired with two of our slipcovered Kate chairs become a cozy breakfast room by the fireplace. The light from a pair of swing arm lamps is perfect for reading the morning newspaper, while the picture light illuminates the collection of vintage cutting boards, artistically displayed on the antique wood beam mantel.

Instead of fabricating new cabinetry, we used antique cupboards for storage. With their worn finishes and lovely imperfections, these case pieces add their own history to Patina Farm.

Although the modern appliances are hidden from view, we left many of the other cooking necessities in plain sight. Well-patinaed copper and stainless steel pots are hung on an unlacquered brass rod above the range, and a collection of wooden spoons and spatulas are stored in an ironstone pitcher on the counter. Small marble shelves on either side of the range offer handy space for oils, teas, and salt and pepper grinders to be displayed. An attractive collection of white bakeware is stacked according to shape on the open shelves of the island, and cutting boards arranged on the mantel become works of art.

Our breakfast table is located next to the fireplace in the kitchen, providing a cozy morning spot for just the two of us, which is becoming a common occurrence now that the children are growing up. The location of the breakfast table also works as a pre-meal gathering spot for guests to enjoy bread, cheese and a glass of wine while dinner is being prepared.

Instead of building new cabinetry, we found an antique French cabinet for storing our dishes and silverware. Although all of our dishes are white, the different shapes and sizes make for an interesting yet restful display.

Creating

We located our offices on the southwest side of our house, where the sun would be bright during the day.

Steve's office has a modern rustic bent. Antique barn beams frame the clean pieces of glass that make up the doors. The asymmetrical stone fireplace is topped by another piece of vintage lumber, and other beams are imbedded in the white plaster ceiling. A neutral palette of warm browns and camels is consistent throughout the space. The only color is provided by the outdoor landscape seen through the sheets of glass and Steve's paintings that hang on the walls.

Steve placed his desk, an old wooden refectory table, across from the fire and close to the glass doors, enabling him to take a quick break from drawing by simply lifting his head and taking in the view. Behind the desk, a room-sized closet provides storage for Steve's oversized printer as well as shelves for material samples and office supplies.

Given his passion for painting, we knew that the materials in Steve's bathroom would need to work well with the supplies of his pastime, so we covered the counter with zinc and used the large Belgian stone sink in this room. Tubes of paint, tins of pastels, metal cups filled with brushes and containers of turpentine are stored on the scaffolding shelves above the counter.

Since Steve would be spending most of his days designing houses as well as painting and drawing in his studio, lighting was key. A rustic chandelier hanging from the ceiling by bronze rods lights the center of the space. Several brass library lights and swing arm fixtures illuminate the artwork on the walls as well as the collections on his shelves. A couple of diminutive table lamps sit on the shelves, adding small pools of light. A vintage industrial task light screws onto the side of his desk, lighting the drawings while he works.

Steve's collections of vintage industrial cogs, plaster pieces, and things of interest also find a home on the scaffolding shelves, adding to the "cabinet of curiosities" vibe.

Steve's office is located in the rustic cedar-covered wing of the house. Antique barn beams frame the clean glass office doors that open to the back garden. Gray painted rebar rods become a simple trellis for the wisteria vines.

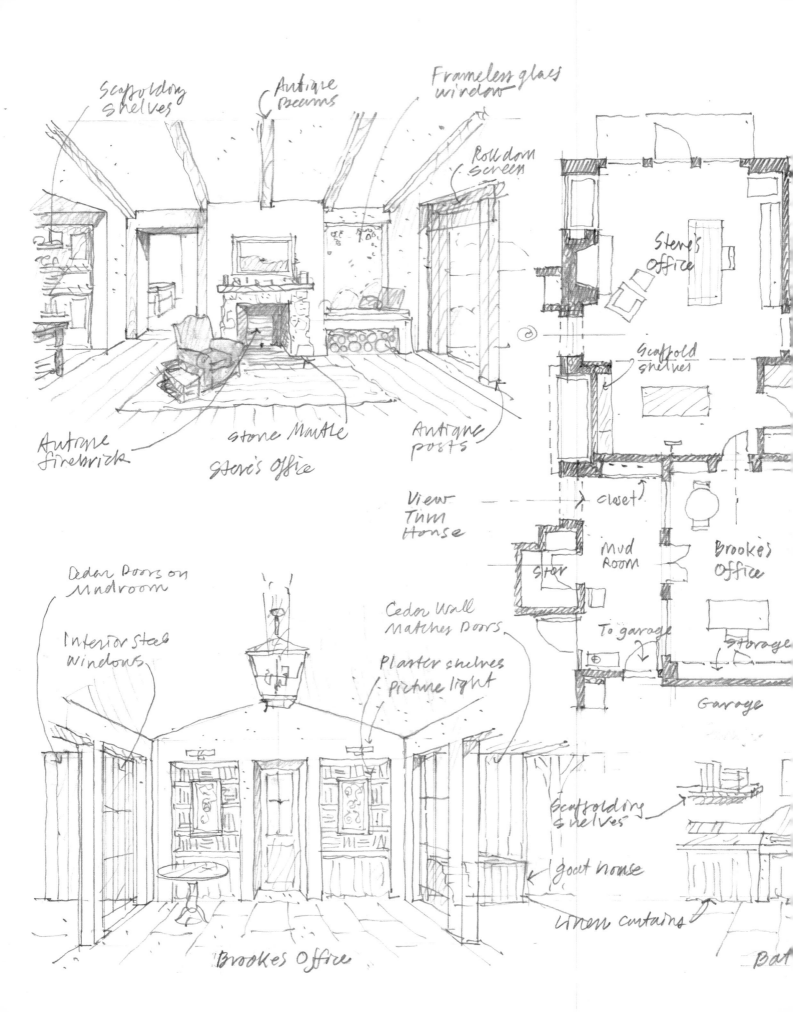

Scaffolding Shelves

Antique Beams

Frameless glass window

Roll down screen

Antique firebrick

Stone Mantle
Steve's Office

Antique posts

View Thm House

Steve's Office

Scaffold shelves

closet

Stair

Mud Room

Brooke's Office

To garage

Storage

Garage

Cedar Doors on Mudroom

Interior Steel Windows

Cedar Wall Matches Doors

Planter shelves

Picture light

Scaffolding Shelves

goat house

Linen curtains

Brookes Office

Bat

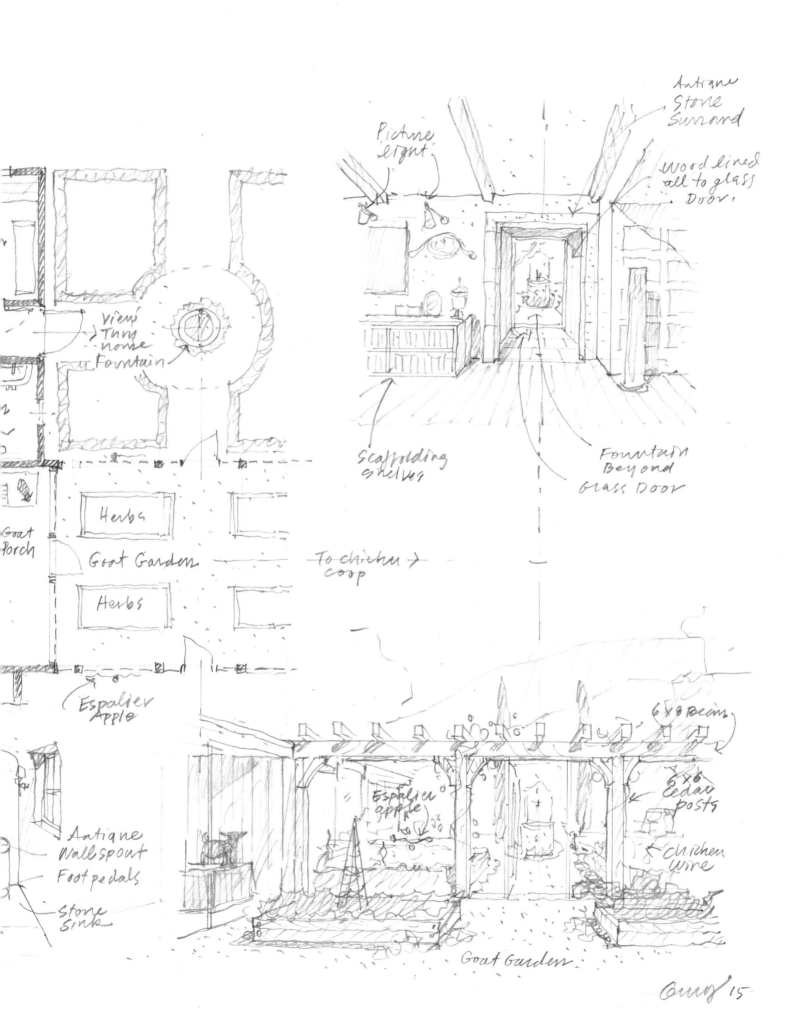

View Thru house Fountain

Goat Porch

Herbs

Goat Garden

Herbs

Espalier Apple

Antique Wallspout
Foot pedals

Stone Sink

Picture light

Antique Stone Surround

Wood lined all to glass Door.

Scaffolding shelves

To chicken coop

Fountain Beyond Glass Door

6 x 8 Beam

Espalier apple

6 x 6 Cedar posts

chicken wire

Goat Garden

Amy/15

The antique stone sink that we discovered in Belgium has a new home in Steve's office bathroom. Foot pedals control the water that flows from the vintage faucet. We wanted the zinc backsplash and countertop to mellow in color, so we left the sheets of zinc outside and watered them with a hose every day for several months during construction.

The 1940s black-and-white photo of Giannetti's Studio and the collections of plaster pieces and paintings displayed on Steve's scaffolding shelves are a reflection of his life story as an artist.

We divided storage into two categories: open shelves for lovely collections and meaningful objects, and hidden storage for the less attractive necessities.

The location of my office allows me to be surrounded by the things I love. As I sit at my desk, I can enjoy a view of my potager garden and the chickens beyond. The goats spend the mornings lazily sprawled out on the cool stone of my porch floor. In the spring and summer, my office is filled with the scent of David Austin roses and lavender.

My office has the feeling of a conservatory. The limestone porch floor runs through my office, and an overscaled rustic lantern hangs from the ceiling in the center of the space. Floor-to-ceiling steel windows were chosen instead of solid walls, adding to the greenhouse feel as well as increasing the natural light and optimizing my views and connection to the gardens. Interior windows balance with those on the porch side and provide a view to the kitchen and the front garden. When standing on the front porch, these interior windows also allow you to see through my office to catch a glimpse of the goats and the potager garden.

Storage was a major concern for my office. I wanted to create an uncluttered room to work while still having plenty of space to house all of my necessary things. My printer and office supplies are hidden behind the set of antique paneled doors we purchased at the French flea market, and storage for other necessities is found on shelves concealed by linen panels. The exposed plaster shelves across from my desk offer display space for my collection of antique books and old pocket watches.

A composition of antique paper and vellum books become artwork on the plaster shelves in my office. Natural linen curtains hide the dog and rabbit supplies.

The set of antique doors that we found in Paris at the Marche Paul Bert are now a paneled focal point. Behind the doors is ample storage for office supplies. The limestone floor in my office flows seamlessly to the goat porch, connecting the two spaces.
<small>ABOVE:</small> *The original cremone bolt opens the doors of my storage area.*

A set of arched gates work as a trellis for the vines on the wall of my porch. A pair of vintage tufted chairs provide a comfortable place to sit and enjoy the garden.
OPPOSITE: *We used the same cedar paneling in the mudroom and on the outside facade of the garages, blurring the line between indoor and outdoor spaces. We throw our car keys in the vintage wooden bowl as we enter the house through the wood-planked garage door.*

Restoring

An antique Swedish clock and vintage chair are placed in the vestibule that leads to our bedroom. Located behind a pair of tall pine doors, this vestibule provides a needed private passage into a bedroom located off the main living space. The linen closet is hidden behind a panel of repurposed wood doors across from the bedroom entrance. The scale of the opening into the bedroom is small, making the entry quite intimate.

Because of the southeast location of our bedroom, we awaken to the softer light of day, and the blush colors of the sunrise slowly fill the room. The plaster walls begin to glow as the light filters in through the glass of the steel doors as well as the modern sheets of glass that are fixed in the east and west walls. The only window treatments are sheer linen panels hung on slender 3/4-inch unlacquered brass rods, which diffuse the light and add to the overall glow.

The clean lines of the architecture are balanced with the rustic textures of an antique limestone mantel and a threadbare rug. Aged gilt, washed teal blue accent pillows and the faded rug, with hints of the pale pinks and blues that can also be found in the sunrise each morning, supply the "barely there" color scheme. The bedding is kept minimal—off-white linen bedding embellished with a few pillows and a shimmery quilt. We felt that a headboard was unnecessary.

The lighting is uncomplicated. The ceiling remains sculptural, without the "pock marks" of recessed lighting. A diminutive antique chandelier fabricated from centuries-old candleholders lights up the center of the room. Sconces and table lamps supply the rest of the ambient light.

Steel doors frame the view of the garden and provide access to the porch. Wood screens pocket into the walls adjacent to the doors, while a small operable panel in the center provides for nighttime ventilation.

The chaise, nestled next to the steel doors, is a piece of our own design, patterned after an antique chase with a smaller, lighter scale than those made today. It is an ideal spot to appreciate the view of the pond, peruse a favorite book, or enjoy a nap with a sleepy pup.

PREVIOUS OVERLEAF: *Steel doors frame the view of the garden and provide access to the porch. Wood screens pocket into the walls adjacent to the doors, while a small operable panel allows for night-time ventilation.* OPPOSITE: *Draperies pocket inside the thickness of the walls, providing the maximum connection to the gardens during the day.*

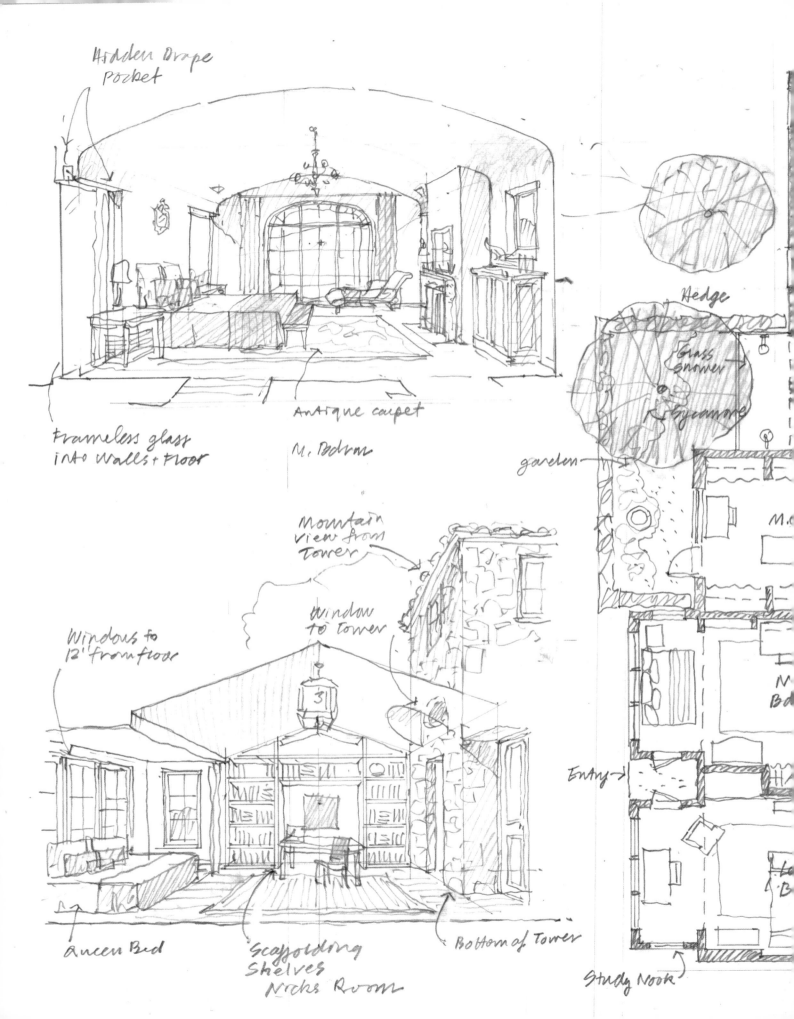

Hidden Drape
Pocket

Frameless glass
into walls + floor

Antique carpet

M. Bodron

Mountain
view from
Tower

Window
to Tower

Windows to
12' from floor

Queen Bed

Scaffolding
Shelves
Nicks Room

Bottom of Tower

Hedge

Glass
Shower

Sycamore

garden

Entry →

Study Nook

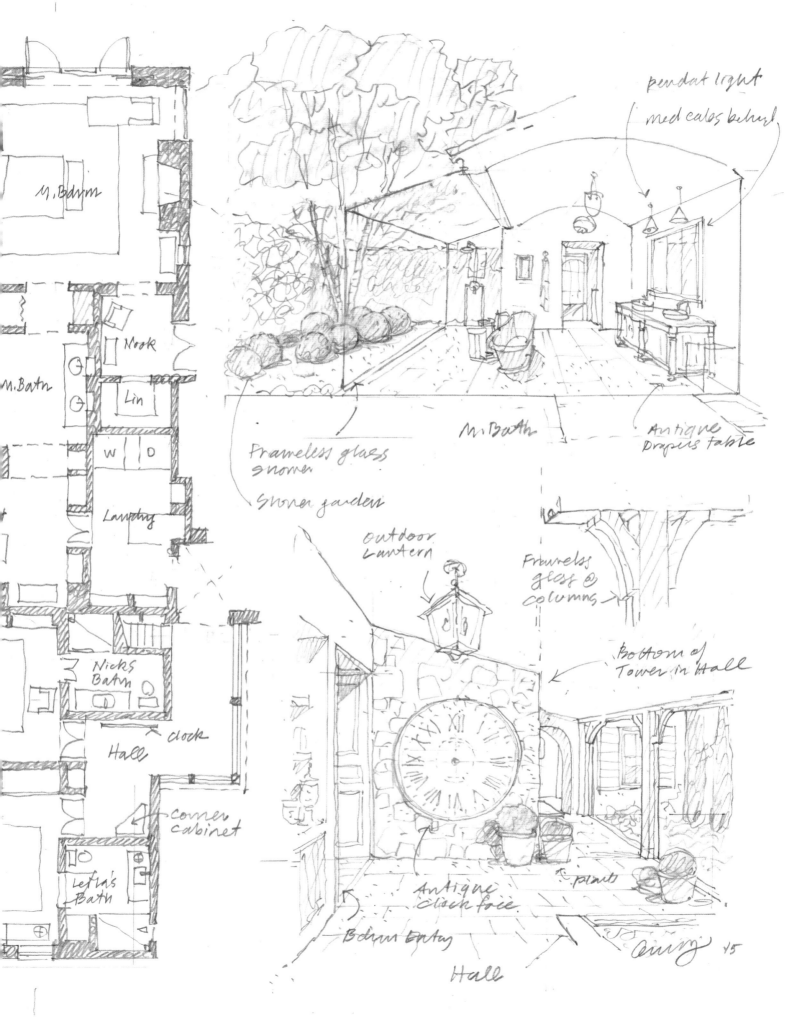

pendat light
med calos behul

M.Bdrm

Nook

Lin

M.Bath

W | D

Landing

M.Bath

Antique
Drapers table

Frameless glass
snower

Snower garden

Frameless
glass @
columns

Bottom of
Tower in Hall

outdoor
Lantern

Nicks
Bath

clock

Hall

corner
cabinet

Antique
Clock face

plants

Leta's
Bath

Bdrm Entry

Hall

45

The faded pink hues of the antique books and the soft blue-gray of our steel doors can also be found in the color palette of the oil painting that hangs in our bedroom. OPPOSITE: *A pair of sconces purchased in Venice, Italy, light up the wall above the antique French limestone mantel.*

The master bathroom is located through an arched plaster doorway adjacent to our bedroom. This glass room evolved from our original idea of a greenhouse bathroom. The monumental sheets of glass that make up the walls and ceiling of our shower allow for an uninterrupted connection to the garden. A small operable panel cut into the glass wall provides ventilation. Shaded by the canopy of the sycamore tree, our bathroom garden is filled with varying sizes of boxwood spheres and blue hydrangea; campanula blankets the ground with pale blue blooms. Tendrils of Virginia Creeper climb the outdoor walls and have begun to make their way across the glass shower roof. Modest lanterns hanging in the branches of the sycamore illuminate the shower in the evening.

A diminutive antique lantern is repurposed as a table lamp. A diminutive window allows a breeze to float through our bedroom as well as providing a peek at the garden as you enter the room. OPPOSITE: *A pair of antique French pine doors open to the vestibule of our master bedroom.*

The unpainted walls have such character and depth as the color varies, depending on their orientation.

Selecting furnishings and materials was key to creating the greenhouse atmosphere we wanted for our bathroom: unlacquered brass plumbing fixtures have a mellow finish; tumbled limestone pavers add an outdoor texture. Antiqued cement column stump side tables become a resting place for soaps. The pewter bathtub sits in the middle of the space, evoking the look of a garden water feature. The draper's table, repurposed as a sink base, has the air of a potting table. The framed mirror above the table houses deep cabinets for all our storage needs, and fabric panels below the table hide additional storage. Although we wanted our bathroom to have the look of a garden, we made sure we wouldn't catch a chill in winter; heated limestone floors and ample heat vents for central air keep our bathroom comfortable all year long.

The lighting fixture selections were inspired by some of our favorite European bathrooms. Over the sinks, two shallow opaque glass shades are suspended by wire covered by twisted braids of fabric. A bell jar lantern, fabricated from a vintage garden cloche, hangs from the ceiling in the center of the room.

Our dressing room is connected to the bathroom. The decoration in this space is kept to a minimum, providing an uncluttered environment to prepare for the beginning and end of the day. Natural linen panels conceal our clothing while keeping it easily accessible. An antique Swedish cabinet in a muted shade of gray provides storage for my sweaters; it is also a focal point when looking through from the master bedroom.

No closet cabinetry was built for our room. Instead, sweaters and purses are stored in a pale gray Swedish cabinet. Other garments are placed on shelves or hangers on rods behind full-height linen draperies.

We tried to use found objects as much as possible in the construction of Patina Farm.
A marble niche discovered at a local marble yard is fitted into the stucco wall of our
shower. OPPOSITE: *The glass wall and ceiling allow the garden to flow into our bathroom.*
Garden elements, including fluted stone columns and boxwood topiaries, further
blur the line between indoor and outdoor space. A dense hedge provides privacy.

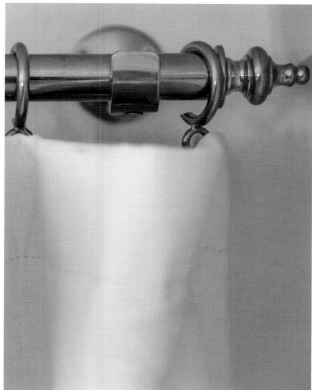

There are only two other pieces of furniture in this area. I placed my vanity in front of the glass doors so I can get ready for my day in the natural light. A sizable tufted burlap bench is perfect for laying out clothing or sitting while putting on boots.

As with all the lighting at Patina Farm, the light fixtures in our dressing area contribute to the serenity of the space. The multi-armed chandelier that hangs in the center of the room supplies ample light, precluding the harsh glare normally offered by recessed ceiling lights. Strip LED lighting illuminates the clothing storage behind the linen panels.

The laundry room is perfectly located next to our dressing room. For ease, the laundry room can be accessed from the closet, through a set of mirrored doors, or from the main space via the small antique door at the end of the vaulted hallway. Knowing I would spend many hours in this room, a lot of thought went into its design so that it would be both pretty and functional. We used the same materials in the laundry room as in the rest of the house. Whitewashed white oak was selected for the substantial counter above the washer and dryer as well as the shelves of the large island. The French limestone floors that flow from the entry hall into the laundry room can tolerate spills and splashes yet still connect the rooms aesthetically. All of the hardware and plumbing fixtures are unlacquered brass, which is aging nicely from the amount of handling it receives.

As in the rest of the house, minimal cabinetry was built for the laundry room; the only two cabinets hang above the washer and dryer. Natural linen panels hide a wall of storage as well as the space underneath the utility sink. Large baskets placed on the island shelves work well for dirty clothes hampers. Smaller baskets on the shelves above the island serve as storage for those one-off socks waiting for their mates to appear.

Lighting and comfort were kept in mind. Similarly to the closet, we used strip LED over counter lighting above the washer and dryer. The rest of the space is lit by ceiling surface-mounted fixtures from Schoolhouse Electric. During the day, a well-placed skylight fills the room with natural light. The operable skylight also allows the hot air to escape. An electric shade can be drawn over the skylight during the hot summer months.

PREVIOUS OVERLEAF: A vintage draper's table is repurposed as our sink base. Large medicine cabinets are housed behind the framed glass mirror. OPPOSITE: Sunlight flows into our dressing room through the large steel windows and door. A tufted burlap bench is the perfect place for putting on shoes or for our pup, Sophie, to rest.

*Inexpensive willow fencing draped over a steel trellis shades the porch off
of our bedroom.* OPPOSITE: *A collection of mossy pots filled with topiaries is
displayed on a vintage steel French garden table in the glassed-in walkway.*

Open wood shelving provides storage in the children's hallway and the
laundry room. Extra blankets and cleaning supplies are hidden behind
the linen draperies. Warm woven baskets are used as hampers.

The location of the children's rooms was given great thought. Although Nick and Leila, our two youngest children, would be living full-time at Patina Farm for a couple of years, we knew that this time would fly by. Separating the children's quarters from the main living spaces allows the house floor plan to expand or contract, depending on the number of us living in the house at any given time.

Nick's room was designed as a library/bedroom. Bookshelves made of repurposed scaffolding planks provided display area for Nick's extensive sneakers collection. When Nick went to college, we gradually turned his room into a design library, filling the shelves with our favorite books. An industrial table that was once Nick's desk is now used as a research space, and his bed has a new life as a reading nook.

Nick's bathroom is located in the base of the bell tower. The scaffolding floorboards and antique timbers of the tower floor also create the ceiling in the bathroom. An industrial console is repurposed as a sink base, and an antique wood door became the frame for his mirror. A Waterworks faucet lifted on a bit of brass pipe serves the vessel sink.

A vibrant blue Swedish side table is used as Leila's sink base. A pendant light replaces the typical sconces and a large vintage mirrored door provides storage for scores of lotions and potions.

In Leila's room, we decided to add some feminine detail in the form of a French-style paneled closet wall. We could not locate antique paneling, so we created the illusion of some by making some panels operable and some fixed. The pale blue-gray of the paneling as well as the chalky colors of the Swedish pieces are compatible for a more mature palette. Vintage sconces fit between the panels, and a petite chandelier hangs from the center of the room.

Both children's rooms have a large nook for their desk that is almost all windows extending nearly to the floor. These areas face east, so the morning light is beautiful in the rooms; the sunlight is nice for waking up as well as getting dressed and ready for the day. The low sills connect the rooms to the garden outside in a way that typical 30-inch-tall windowsills could never do. The desks simply overlap the windows. The glass nooks can be closed off from the sleeping portion of the rooms by large floor-to-ceiling drapes.

A Swedish corner cabinet, stripped to show the original hues of the pine material, is used for display and storage in the children's vestibule.

OPPOSITE: *A wall of shelves built with scaffolding boards are filled with books, giving Nick's room a cozy library aesthetic.* ABOVE: *A metal industrial table becomes Nick's sink base. An antique wood frame surrounds the mirror that hides his medicine cabinet. The plumbing below the sink is left exposed, adding to the industrial atmosphere of the bathroom.*

An antique Swedish side table works as Leila's sink base. A linen skirt hides extra storage below. A simple pendant light hangs on one side of the sink, balanced by a robe hook on the opposite side. The 30-inch-tall table works well with the vessel sink. Because the table was also a bit shallow, we used a wall mount faucet.

OPPOSITE: *Leila's Swedish desk is placed in front of the tall windows. Hidden screens pull down from the top of each window. Keeping the windowsill low to the ground visually connects Leila's room to her garden, while a French door gives her access to her own secret rose garden.*
ABOVE: *An antique sconce is a touch of elegance on Leila's clean paneled closet wall.*

Rejuvenating

Living in the mild climate of Ojai, with all of its natural beauty, we regard the gardens that surround our house as outdoor rooms, spaces that are connected to the indoor areas of the house both visually and aesthetically. They were designed in the same manner as the indoor rooms. Studying floor plans, furniture layouts, and material selections, we ensured that each space works for the activities that will take place. We considered focal points, vistas and the various scaled elements in each outdoor room.

Similarly to the spaces inside the house, we have limited our outside color palette as well as the different species of plant materials in order to achieve a calm atmosphere. Closer to the house, the outdoor spaces are more formal: a parterre garden filled with David Austin roses and companion plants, a boxwood garden comprised of clipped boxwood spheres of varying sizes. Farther from the house, the plantings become more relaxed and natural as they blend with the existing foliage.

All of the five senses are taken into consideration; we also focus on the textures, scents, sounds, and in some of the gardens, taste, as well as visual attractiveness.

As you enter the front door, there is a clear view through the home. Only the glass-and-steel door at the back of the house separates you from the garden beyond. The sight and sound of the limestone fountain draws your eye through the house to the boxwood garden. This space mirrors the indoor living and dining areas, and when the weather allows, we open all of the doors and windows to create one large indoor/outdoor room We placed a wooden farmhouse table surrounded by a set of garden chairs underneath the stately oak tree for shady outdoor dining. The sizable kitchen windows allow for easy pass-through of food and drinks.

We placed a free-form fire pit reminiscent of a casual campfire next to the outdoor dining room. The fire pit is surrounded by two faux bois armchairs and an L-shaped upholstered built-in sofa covered with pale blue toss pillows and cozy throw blankets. This comfortable lounge

We decided to place the pond on the lower portion of our property. In that location, the pond becomes a destination as well as a serene water element to view from inside the main house and guesthouse. The pond has also become home to a family of ducks as well as what sounds like a hundred vocal frogs!

donkey barn

shed

greenhouse

lawn

Fruit Trees

Roses

Rose Trellis

vege garden

mini donkeys

Lavender maze

Entry gate

Motor
Court

Drive

Fountain

Mr Bath
garden

goats
Waterfall

Guest house

Dock

Boat

Aug '15

The arms of the monumental oak tree define our outdoor dining room.

space is the perfect after-dinner hangout where we share laughter and stories with our friends and family as our faces are lit by the glow of the fire.

A scented French lavender–lined path leads down to the pond. Seen from the house, the pond becomes a reflective focal point as well as a beautiful destination. It also serves as a repository for all of the water drainage on the property. A variety of wildlife has found a home here. During different times of the year, ducks flock to the pond to enjoy the cool water and make nests in the tall grasses. Our floating duck house is another favorite place for ducks to gather, safe from the on-shore predators. Local frogs and even a stray turtle now find safe housing here as well.

The pond is its own ecosystem. Water hyacinth and cattail add visual beauty while aerating the pond. Mosquito fish keep the mosquito population down as well as providing food for the birds; the fish reproduce pretty quickly, so we don't need to replenish them.

Three of the most structured garden areas are located next to our offices, on the west side of the house. The beauty and aroma of the formal rose garden can be enjoyed from both offices. We filled the beds with my favorite David Austin roses: the pale peach 'A Shropshire Lad' and the deeper peach-hued 'Ambridge Rose' share space with an array of pink beauties, including 'Abraham Darby,' 'Evelyn,' 'Wildeve' and 'Heritage.'

Sprinkled among the rose bushes are several ground covers, including a variety of fluttery geraniums, silver lambs ear, and delicate Santa Barbara daisies. We planted a few peach-colored bearded irises that put on quite a show in early spring. In lieu of the traditional boxwood hedging, we chose a more casual hedge of germander.

We visually connected the rose garden to the inside of the house in a couple of ways. The well fountain in the center of the parterre is on axis with the large glass door in Steve's office. It's a beautiful focal point when looking through the house. The limestone hallway blends with the color of the exterior gravel, blurring the line between the indoor and outdoor spaces.

The kumquat trees add a pop of color to the back garden.
Apparently they are delicious as well.

We used a variety of light fixtures on the exterior of the house. An antique lantern is hung on the wood wall of Steve's office. With its ever-changing foliage, the Virginia creeper provides a sense of the seasons throughout the year. OPPOSITE: *The lounging area around the fire pit is the popular hangout after dinner.*

Sharing

One of our dreams for Patina Farm was that it would become a place for our family and friends to visit and share in the world that we created, a place where our children would bring their children to play with the animals and swim in the pond. We located the guest quarters on the east end of the property, nestled next to the three-hundred-year-old oak tree. Through the trees, guests have a view of the ducks swimming on the pond as well as the donkeys grazing below. A parking space is conveniently located next to the little house, allowing people to come and go as they please.

We gave the guesthouse the story of an "artist studio," which enabled us to create a rustic space populated with collections. We filled an eighteenth-century Italian cabinet with an array of the ornamental plaster pieces from Giannetti's Studio. The walls are covered in vintage landscapes found at local antique stores. Other found treasures and oddities share space with the dishes on the scaffolding shelves in the kitchenette.

Aesthetically, we wanted the guesthouse to have the feel of the rustic wings of the house, with a facade of weathered-gray-stained cedar and a standing seam galvanized metal roof. Similarly as in Steve's office, large single-paned glass doors framed in antique timbers open to view. Antique timbers also add warmth to the space as ceiling beams and the mantel of the asymmetrical limestone fireplace. Scaffolding planks are used as shelving material in the kitchenette, and an informal iron chandelier lights the space. Natural linen draperies are used throughout the guesthouse, providing privacy as well as hiding the kitchen pantry storage.

The furnishings are neutral; a natural linen slipcovered sofa and a pair of vintage leather chairs around an oversized ottoman create the main seating area, while two of our leather Frasier chairs, paired with an antique English side table, work well as a place to eat by the view. A thick-piled

PREVIOUS OVERLEAF: *Our guests enjoy the calming scent of the lavender as they walk along the gravel path towards the guesthouse.* OPPOSITE: *We placed rose vines in various locations to frame the views from the house and as focal points. We enjoy this Pearly Gates rose vine from our bedroom windows.*

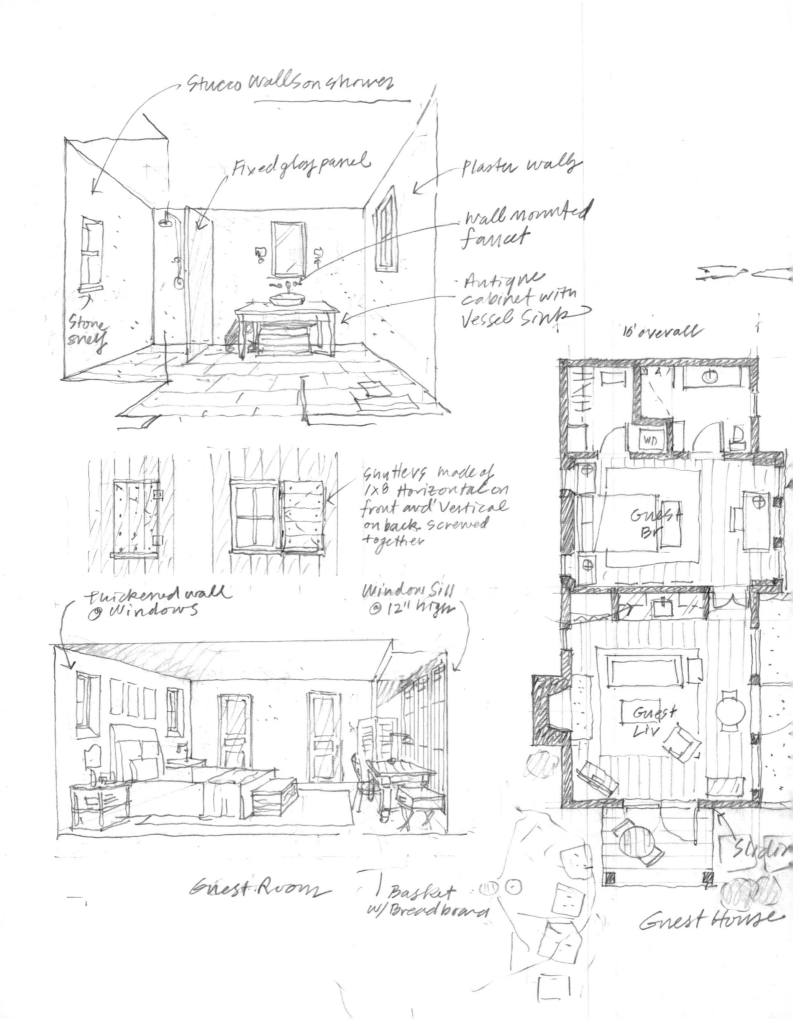

Stucco Walls on shower

Fixed glass panel

Plaster walls

Wall mounted faucet

Antique cabinet with vessel sink

Stone shelf

Shutters made of 1x8 Horizontal on front and vertical on back. screwed together

Thickened wall @ windows

Window sill @ 12" high

16' overall

WD

Guest Br

Guest Liv

Guest Room

Basket w/ Breadboard

Shutters

Guest House

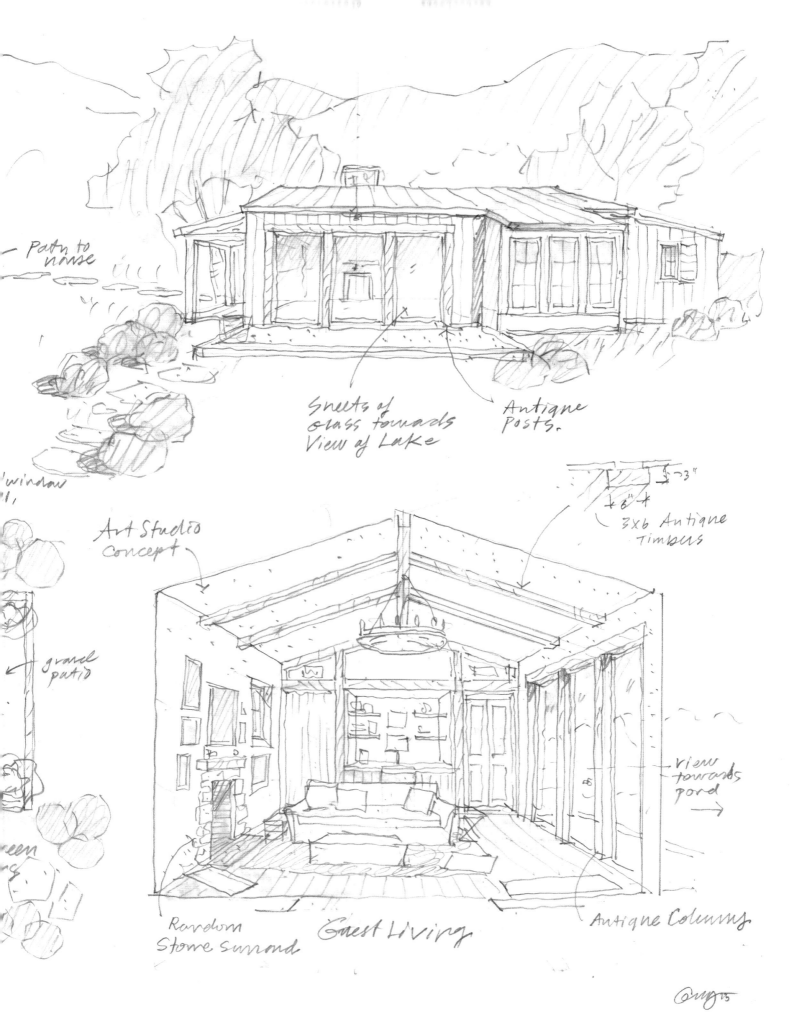

Path to house

Sheets of glass towards View of Lake

Antique Posts.

window

Art Studio Concept

gravel patio

3x6 Antique Timbers

view towards pond

Random Stone Surround

Guest Living

Antique Columns

An antique Italian cabinet with embossed leather interior is used for storage in the main space of the guesthouse. OPPOSITE: *Three large glass doors allow our visitors to enjoy the view of the pond as well as the donkeys playing in the lower field.*

Moroccan area rug and pillows covered in a mix of indigo vintage fabrics add soft textures. It's a wonderful space filled with natural light that streams into the room from three sides.

The bedroom is entered through a pair of antique pine doors. The same natural linen that is used for the window treatments also covers the headboard. A blue-and-white-striped rug, soft cotton blanket and blue vintage textile pillows add some pops of color.

An antique bleached oak table is paired with a vintage leather office chair next to the windows of the guest bedroom. OPPOSITE: *In the main space of the guesthouse, antique barn beams frame the kitchen, and tall linen draperies cover the pantry storage. The seating area is a mix of antique chairs and our Courtney sofa, dressed in vintage textile pillows.*

A Swedish desk is used as the sink base. A basket is the perfect place to store extra towels. OPPOSITE: *Steve's tonal paintings provided the inspiration for the color palette of the guest bedroom. Vintage Japanese textile pillows and a soft cotton woven blanket add texture to the natural linen bed. A unique vintage industrial light with its original cloth-covered wiring is now an artistic bedside lamp.*

Farming

When we first dreamed of living on Patina Farm, we imagined that we would spend our free time tending to the gardens and the animals. We envisioned eating our chickens' fresh eggs in the morning and cooking with the vegetables and fruits we would grow. To make these dreams come true, we first needed to design and build the gardens and animal structures.

During the time when we were designing Patina Farm, we took our children on a trip to visit colleges back East. To break up the many campus tours, we decided to visit George Washington's Mount Vernon. Upon arrival, we were disappointed to discover seemingly never-ending lines of visitors waiting to enter the various buildings, so we decided to walk around the gardens. What a wonderful unexpected bounty of inspiration! George Washington was the epitome of the gentleman farmer. His gardens were the perfect combination of beautiful form and function. Each garden had a formal structure combined with a relaxed, unpretentious air. We were impressed by Washington's ability to create a self-sustaining farm with such charm.

We made note of the different elements from Mount Vernon that we wanted to emulate at Patina Farm, from small details like the rows of espaliered fruit trees on simple wood trellises to larger design ideas like the symmetrical axial compositions of the gardens. I noticed the way irises and tulips shared space with the lettuce and cabbages in the vegetable garden. The natural twigs used for the sweet pea supports were both practical and attractive. Even the most rustic structures, like Dung Repository, with its gray wooden board walls, log columns and shingle roof, inspired our color palette as well as helping us decide to create our own compost area.

After our trip, we began to compile more inspiration for our gardens and animal areas. I focused on the smaller details, while Steve figured out how the different areas would relate to each other. One of the first animal structures we designed was the chicken coop. Its proximity to my office meant that it needed to be beautiful to look at as well as provide impenetrable

Since we can see Daisy and Buttercup roaming in the field below the house, we are often enticed to stop work in the middle of the day to enjoy some time with them.

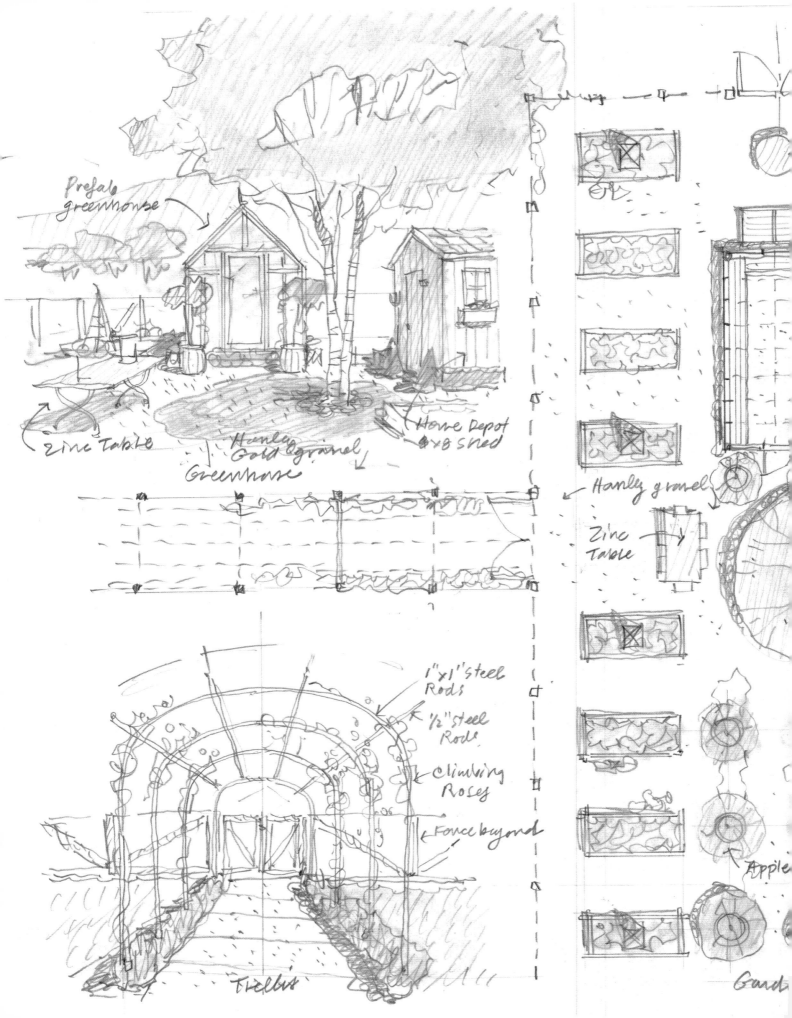

Prefab greenhouse

Zinc Table

Hanley Gold Gravel
Greenhouse

Home Depot 8x8 shed

Hanley gravel

Zinc Table

1"x1" steel Rods

½" steel Rods

Climbing Roses

Fence beyond

Apple

Trellis

Gard

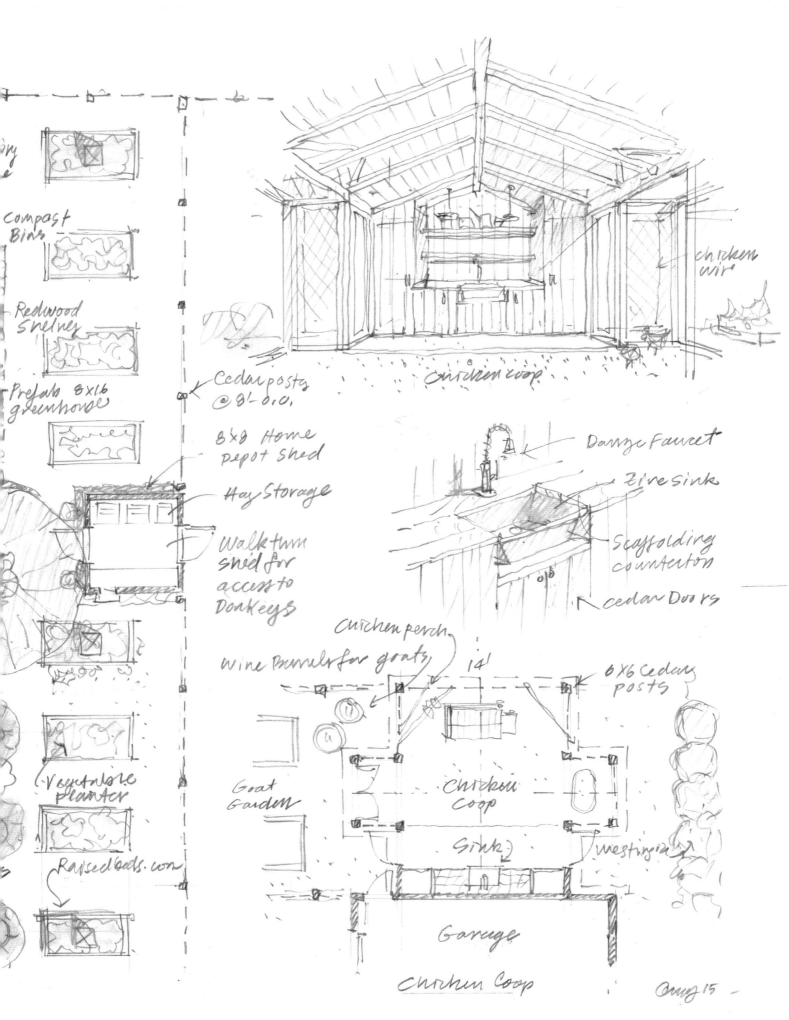

compost
Bins

Redwood
shelves

Prefab 8x16
greenhouse

Cedar posts
@ 8'-0.0.

8x8 Home
Depot Shed

Hay Storage

Walk thru
shed for
access to
Donkeys

Vegetable
planter

Raisedbeds.com

chicken
wire

Chicken coop

Danze Faucet

Zinc sink

Scaffolding
countertop

cedar Doors

Chicken perch

Wine Barrel for goats

14'

6x6 cedar
posts

Goat
Garden

Chicken
Coop

Sink

westinghe

Garage

Chicken Coop

aug 15

I always knew that Patina Farm would be populated with animals. As they roam our property, the donkeys, goats and chickens make Patina Farm come alive!

protection for our brood. The coop was designed as a pavilion wing off of the farthest garage "barn" structure. Like the garage, the coop was made of gray-stained cedar planks with a galvanized standing seam metal roof. A vintage metal cupola found a home on the roof, directly across from its mate on the roof of my office.

The coop is a symmetrical structure, with a pair of double doors on axis with the double doors of my office. Two narrower wings give the coop its T shape. Inside is a "chicken kitchen." No, we do not prepare chicken for our dinner; having named all of them, eating them is out of the question! Instead, this area is used to care for the chickens. I can fill the chickens' watering container with fresh water and clean their food containers in the sink, fabricated from a vintage galvanized garden trough. The cabinets provide ample storage for extra feed, bedding material and chicken treats. The small refrigerator stores their eggs. My collection of vintage watering cans is displayed on shelves above the scaffolding counter.

Inside the larger coop, we have placed the chicken house that we brought from Santa Monica. Inside the chicken house are several nesting boxes and places for the chickens to roost. The upper part of the house also provides the smaller chickens a cozy place to sleep, while the larger ones prefer to spend their evenings on the wooden poles installed in the corners of the coop about five feet above the ground. Because predatory animals are abundant in Ojai, we need to make sure the coop is secure. We placed steel mesh underneath the coop to ensure no burrowing animals could dig into the coop. The chicken wire walls and the locked doors keep the coyotes at bay.

After living at Patina Farm for about six months, we began to expand the cultivated areas of our land. The arrival of Daisy and Buttercup, our donkeys, signaled it was time to build an area for them to live. Since the other farm structures were situated on the west side of our property, we placed the donkey enclosure on the west as well. The donkey enclosure was the first developed area on the lower portion of the land and began the process of achieving our goal to utilize all parts of the property.

The donkey area is simple in design. We used the same fencing material as the perimeter fence, consisting of galvanized mesh fencing material between split rail verticals. We turned a Home Depot storage shed into a charming donkey house by staining it gray and adding an oversized cupola to the roof. Instead of using the doors at the front of the shed, we pushed them back and built a partitioned area, perfect for storing hay and donkey harnesses.

The goats have taken over the little garden next to my office. Because this garden is gated and fenced, it is a safe place for them to spend their evenings.

The wood trellis that surrounds the goat garden frames the view of the antique well fountain in the center of the David Austen rose garden. The pair of cypress trees leads your eye to the view beyond. OPPOSITE: A vintage galvanized trough was used as the sink in the chicken coop. The scaffolding shelves work well for displaying my collection of vintage watering cans. A refrigerator for extra eggs is hidden behind the wood door to the right of the sink.

When the donks were young, they were very content in their 90' x 90' enclosure. They spent their days chasing each other and resting next to their house in the shade of the large California pepper tree. But as they matured, Daisy and Buttercup started braying loudly at 4:00 in the morning, giving us a strong hint that we needed to make a change. We tried a few different modifications—feeding them earlier, using a slow feeder so they would eat slower, putting toys in their pen—but nothing seemed to stop the too early wake-up call. Then one day we decided to let them out of their pen to graze the entire property—no more braying!

Unfortunately, Daisy and Buttercup were also doing a great deal of damage to the gardens that surround our house. We needed to create an elegant solution to keep them on the bottom portion of the land. With this in mind, we started to design the gardens that would populate this lower acreage. These gardens would solve our donkey destruction issue as well as give us a destination, an excuse to visit the bottom portion of our land. Like Washington's Mt. Vernon, our new gardens have a casual feel, but the underlying design has symmetry and axial composition. The design consists of several large-scale elements, comprised of the potager, rose-covered trellis and lavender labyrinth.

Our potager at Patina Farm is the realization of the dream that began with our small kitchen garden in Santa Monica. We now have twenty raised planter beds—ample room to grow a bounty of vegetables, herbs and seasonal flowers. We purchased our mortis-and-tenon raised beds online from The Farmstead. Sturdy, inexpensive and easy to assemble, these cedar planter beds quickly age to a beautiful silver gray. We attached chicken wire to the bottom of each planter to keep our produce safe from burrowing gophers and ground squirrels. We also installed drip irrigation in each box for watering ease and conservation.

The vegetable garden is sited on the lower portion of our property, in clear view of the kitchen windows. This new garden sits next to the donkey enclosure, and Daisy and Buttercup always come to visit when they see me gardening. I reward them for their companionship with carrots grown in the garden. Of course, our three curious goats follow me down to the garden as well, and I can't resist inviting them in for a nibble every now and again.

In the middle of the potager, a group of apple trees line the gravel pathway that leads to the greenhouse. These ornamental fruit trees provide a row of mid-level height elements and add

We limited our garden color palette to shades of white, pink and lavender. Santa Barbara daisies, ceanothus and purple geraniums are lovely companions for my David Austin roses.

linear structure to the garden. The choice of vintage wine barrels as planters contributes to the casual air of this formal composition.

The greenhouse is the main focal point of the vegetable garden. We modified a redwood Mt. Rainier greenhouse, fabricated by Sunshine, raising it up on a foundation of heavy cedar timbers. This extra height gives the greenhouse more presence when looking at it from our house above. The redwood counter and shelves that wrap around three sides of the interior of the greenhouse supply plenty of space for seedlings to grow during the chilly days of winter, as well as providing space for storage of seeds, soil and pots. The same globe string lights that we use in the goat garden also illuminate the greenhouse. A miniature hedge of rosemary is planted around the greenhouse, adding some structured greenery.

A smaller 8' x 8' Home Depot garden shed is placed on axis with the center of the donkey enclosure. The shed is the perfect size to store extra hay as well as larger garden tools and soil. We modified the shed by adding a door to the back, allowing us to access the hay from the donkey enclosure. Another miniature rosemary hedge is planted around the shed, and two cone-shaped rosemary topiaries flank the front door.

The greenhouse and garden shed combined with the sycamore tree growing nearby define a smaller space within the vegetable garden. We turned this area into a shady outdoor dining spot. The zinc-top table, which was once our main dining table, doubles beautifully as a potting table as well. The tree is lit from below as well as from several small hanging copper lanterns on the limbs.

On axis with the center of the new vegetable garden, a series of rose-covered arches shades a gravel pathway that leads to a maze of lavender. Lavender also lines the pathway, obscuring the view of a mesh fence that runs the entire length of the pathway and the back of the lavender maze. The fence subtly allows us to keep the donkeys on the back acreage of our property, where there is plenty of room to graze without destroying the cultivated gardens.

One of the main reasons that we built Patina Farm was to show our children the power of a dream. We've always told our children that dreams can come true. Yes, their fulfillment requires a lot of hard work and determination, but they are attainable.

Champagne grape vines climb the wire of the chicken coop,
providing shade as well as a tasty treat for the chickens!

OPPOSITE: *Shaded by the sycamore tree, a long table is the perfect place to snack on the fruits and vegetables harvested from the garden. For some added quirkiness, we placed vintage cupolas on the top of the chicken coop and the little donkey shed.*

OPPOSITE: *An antique oil jar invites your eye to the end of the rose-covered trellis. Spanish lavender lines the gravel path and circles the olive jar.*

We fitted the prefabricated greenhouse with two rows of shelves for protecting delicate plants during the winter and starting seedlings in early spring. An allée of Fuji apple trees planted in vintage wine barrels adds some mid-level height elements to the garden.

Our family enjoyed the challenge of eating the abundant crops we grew this year. Multicolored kale, lettuces and onions as well as the espaliered apples are both beautiful and delicious.

One of the main reasons that we built Patina Farm was to show our children the power of a dream. We've always told our children that dreams can come true. Yes, their fulfillment requires a lot of hard work and determination, but they are attainable. We have been fortunate to have clients that believe this as well.

Resources

Giannetti Home
11980 San Vicente Blvd., Ste. 101
Los Angeles, CA 90049
www.GiannettiHome.com

ANTIQUES AND ARCHITECTURAL ELEMENTS

Atelier de Campagne
15 Mountain View Rd.
Corralitos, CA 95076
infoatelierdc@gmail.com

We first discovered Atelier de Campagne at the Alameda Flea Market. Owners Trinidad Castro and Johan de Meulenaere import unique items from Europe, including beautifully worn shutters, garden elements, and antique furniture.

A. Tyner
425 Peachtree Hills Ave.
Building 2, #13
Atlanta, GA 30305
www.swedishantiques.biz
404.367.4484

A. Tyner has a huge selection of Swedish and French antique furniture and architectural elements. They are a pleasure to work with.

Jacqueline Adams
425 Peachtree Hills Ave., Ste. 7
Atlanta, GA 30305
www.JacquelineAdamsAntiques.com

A great resource for European antiques.

Alexandra
156 King St.
Charleston, SC 29401
www.AlexandraFrenchAntiques.com

Beautifully edited Swedish antiques.

AM Designs
Showroom
Albert Claudestraat 21
2018 Antwerp
Belgium
www.amDesigns.com

Located in Belgium, owner Mark Mertens procures a selection of rustic European antiques with a Belgian aesthetic.

A Beautiful Mess
28861 West Agoura Rd.
Agoura Hills, CA 91301
www.abeautifulmessantiques.com

Owner Kymberley Fraser fills her store with fantastic one-of-a-kind industrial, primitive and European antiques.

Agoura Antique Market
28863 West Agoura Rd.
Agoura Hills, CA 91301
818.706.8366
www.agouraantiquemart.com

The ever-changing displays are always filled with unique vintage pieces. We found the cupola for the donkey shed here as well as smaller items for our home.

Big Daddy's Antiques
3334 La Cienega Pl.
Los Angeles, CA 90016

1550 17th St.
San Francisco, CA 94107
www.bdantiques.com

One of our favorite resources for vintage leather chairs, industrial, garden, and architectural elements. Owner Shane Brown travels around the world to find unique one-of-a-kind pieces.

C'est la Vie
565 Westlake St.
Suite 300A
Encinitas, CA 92024
www.cestlavieantiques.com

Owner Sara Wardrip imports containers of gorgeous European antiques several times a year.

Eloquence
3601 Holdrege Ave.
Los Angeles, CA 90016
www.eloquenceinc.com

Owners Amelia and Kim Redmond travel the globe in search of antique and vintage pieces. They have also created several beautiful European-inspired furniture lines.

Exquisite Surfaces
289 N. Robertson Blvd.
Beverly Hills, CA 90211
www.xsurfaces.com

A fantastic resource for antique building materials, including limestone mantels, terra-cotta roof tiles, and European wood floors.

Foxgloves Antiques
699 Miami Cir.
Atlanta, GA 30324
www.foxgloveantiques.com

An excellent antique collective comprised of more than a dozen international dealers.

Giannetti's Studios
3806 38th St.
Brentwood, MD 20722
301.927.0033

Beautiful plaster ornament and molding.

M. Naeve
1911 Westheimer Rd.
Houston, TX 77098
www.mnaeve.com

Owner Margaret Naeve imports a rustic yet elegant selection of European antiques.

Marston Luce
1651 Wisconsin Ave. NW
Washington, DC 20007
www.marstonluce.com

Specializing in French and Swedish antiques.

Michel Verschaeve
Brugsesteenweg 362
8520 Kuume
Belgium
+32 (0)56 704690
www.verschaevenv.be

Michel Verschaeve has filled an enormous warehouse with an array of European antique building materials. We purchased most of our interior doors, as well as our stone quatre foils, from Michel Verschaeve.

L&K Antiques
Vaxjovagen 525, 343 74 Liatorp
Sweden
www.gustafssonhb.com

Located in the rural south of Sweden, L&K Antiques focuses on Scandinavian 18th- and 19th-century furniture and antiques. Their specialty is wonderfully restored gustation and rococo painted furniture.

Lee Stanton
769 N. La Cienega Blvd.
Los Angeles, CA 90069
www.leestanton.com

Antiquarian Lee Stanton's inventory is an eclectic mix of 17th-, 18th-, and 19th-century British and European antiques.

Lief
646 N. Almont Dr.
Los Angeles, CA 90069
www.liefalmont.com

Swedish brothers Stefan and Michael Aarestrup have created something special. Each piece they select is a piece of art, whether it is Swedish baroque or ancient Chinese.

Lucca Antiques
744 N. La Cienega Blvd.
Los Angeles, CA 90069

306 E. 61st St., 4th Fl.
New York, NY 10065

111 Rhode Island St., Ste. F
San Francisco, CA 94103
www.luccaantiques.com

Lucca Antiques showrooms express the owners' appreciation for antiques and architectural elements as well as "their passion for creating their own designs from old materials and found objects."

Tara Shaw
1526 Religious St.
New Orleans, LA 70130
www.tarashaw.com

Owner Tara Shaw is both curator of fine antiques and creator of a lovely reproduction European furniture line.

Tone on Tone
7920 Woodmont Ave.
Bethesda, MD 20814
www.tone-on-tone.com

Owners Loi Thai and Thomas Troeschel have created a fantastic resource for 18th- and 19th-century painted Swedish antiques, as well as creamware, white ironstone and garden furnishings.

Vintage Timberworks
47100 Rainbow Canyon Rd.
Temecula, CA 92592
www.vintagetimber.com

The people at Vintage Timberworks helped us select the perfect reclaimed beams for Patina Farm.

GARDEN

Botanik
2329 Lillie Ave.
Summerland, CA 93067
www.botanikinc.com

A wonderful home and garden store filled with vintage finds, as well as succulent gardens, boxwood topiaries and unique accessories.

The Farmstead
527 Meetinghouse Rd.
South Chatham, MA 02659
www.gardenraisedbeds.com

Reasonably priced, easily constructed raised garden beds.

Flora Gardens Nursery
245 Baldwin Rd.
Ojai, CA 93023
www.floragardens.net

Our wonderful local nursery.

Rose Story Farm
Carpinteria, CA
805.566.4885
www.rosestoryfarm.com

Owner Danielle Dall'Armi has been honored with the Great Rosarian of the World award for good reason! Rose Story Farm is one of the most charming farms I've ever visited — and it's filled with over 25,000 rose bushes of more than 120 varieties. If you are in the Carpinteria area, you must carve out some time for a tour.

Ricardo Gutierrez Landscape
805.698.9055

Patina Farm would not be nearly as beautiful without the hard work of Ricardo and his team. They maintain all of the gardens and installed the new potager.

TEXTILES

Claremont Furnishing Fabrics
723 N. La Cienega Blvd.
Los Angeles, CA 90069
www.claremontfurnishing.com

Wholesale showroom specializing in European textiles and trimmings.

D. Bryant Archie
260 W. 35th St., Ste. 200
New York, NY 10001
www.dbryantarchie.com

Our favorite Alpaca pillows and throws.

Jamal's Rug Collection
657 N. La Cienega Blvd.
West Hollywood, CA 90069
310.289.9777

I visit Jamal whenever I'm looking for that perfect threadbare, faded antique rug.

Libeco Linen
230 Fifth Ave., Ste. 1300
New York, NY 10001
www.libeco.com

True Belgian linen in fantastic weathered and muted colors.

DeLany & Long
Peg Winship at Rogers and Goffigon
41 Chestnut Street
Greenwich, CT 06830
www.delanyandlong.com
206.618.4145

Lovely fabrics, trims and sheers in our favorite pale color palette.

Thomas Lavin
Pacific Design Center
8687 Melrose Ave., Ste. B310
West Hollywood, CA 90069
www.thomaslavin.com

My resource for some of my favorite textiles, including C&C Milano, Travers & Co., Hodsoll McKenzie and de Le Cuona.

PLUMBING FIXTURES

Waterworks
Viktoria Urabanas
8580 Melrose Ave.
West Hollywood, CA 90069
www.waterworks.com
vurbanas@waterworks.com

The most gorgeous plumbing fixtures. They are truly jewelry for the bathroom.

Barber Wilsons
Crawley Road,
Wood Green,
London. N22 6AH,
United Kingdom
www.barwil.co.uk

Their kitchen faucets are the perfect proportions.

Newport Brass
2001 Carnegie Ave.
Santa Ana, CA 92705
www.newportbrass.com

A less expensive unlacquered brass alternative.

ANIMAL RESOURCES

Amber Waves
1320 Mountain Ave.
Norco, CA 92860
www.amberwaves.info

Owners Debbie and Jim thoughtfully breed Bearded Silkie Bantam chickens, African Pygmy Goats and Pyrenean Mountain dogs.

Seein' Spots Farm
2599 Baseline Ave.
Solvang, CA 93463
www.seeinspotsfarm.com

We purchased all four of our adorable miniature Sicilian donkeys from Linda Marchi. She is caring and very patient with us first-time donkey owners.

Acknowledgments

We extend heartfelt gratitude to all of the talented people who helped us create this book:

To Jill Cohen, our dear friend and book agent, for guiding us through the process from the beginning, when Patina Farm was just a dream, to the realization of this book.

To Doug Turshen and Steve Turner for their expert guidance through the design process of this book.

To our wonderful friend Clinton Smith for his memorable visits and for truly understanding why we love Patina Farm.

To Madge Baird, our editor at Gibbs Smith, for her patience and support of our vision.

To Lisa Romerein and her assistant Matt Harbicht for capturing the beauty of Patina Farm.

Special appreciation to our *Velvet and Linen* readers and Instagram followers for sharing this journey with us.

20 19 18 17 16   5 4 3 2 1

Published by
Gibbs Smith
P.O. Box 667
Layton, Utah 84041

1.800.835.4993 orders
www.gibbs-smith.com

Designed by Doug Turshen with Steve Turner
Printed and bound in China

Gibbs Smith books are printed on either recycled, 100% post-consumer waste, FSC-certified papers
or on paper produced from sustainable PEFC-certified forest/controlled wood source. Learn more at
www.pefc.org.

Library of Congress Cataloging-in-Publication Data

Giannetti, Brooke, author.
  Patina Farm / Brooke Giannetti & Steve Giannetti. — First Edition.
    pages cm
  ISBN 978-1-4236-4046-2
1. Architecture, Domestic—California—Ojai Valley—History—21st century. 2. Interior
decoration—California—Ojai Valley—History—21st century. 3. Giannetti, Steve—Homes and
haunts—California—Ojai Valley. 4. Giannetti, Brooke—Homes and haunts—California—Ojai Valley.
I. Giannetti, Steve, author. II. Title.
  NA737.G485A4 2016
  728'.60979492—dc23
                        2015030394

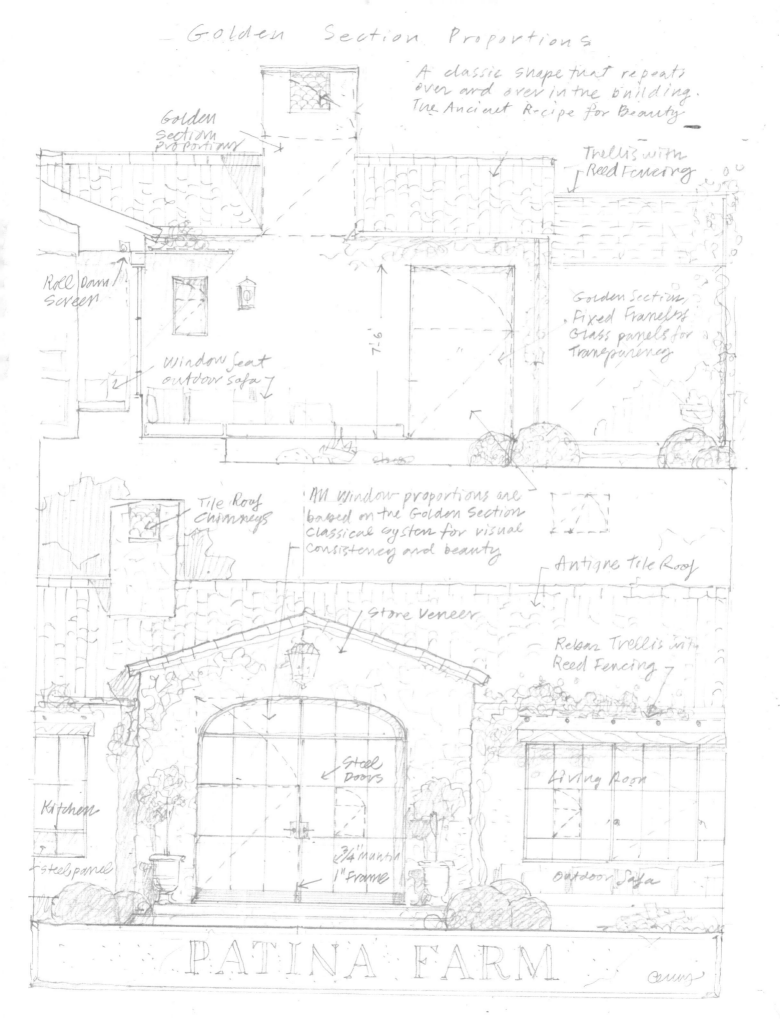

Golden Section Proportions

A classic shape that repeats over and over in the building. The Ancient Recipe for Beauty

Golden Section proportions

Trellis with Reed Fencing

Roll Down Screen

Golden Section Fixed Frameless Glass panels for Transparency

Window Seat outdoor sofa

7'-6"

Tile Roof Chimneys

All Window proportions are based on the Golden Section classical system for visual consistency and beauty

Antique Tile Roof

Stone Veneer

Rebar Trellis with Reed Fencing

Steel Doors

Living Room

Kitchen

Steel panel

¾" Muntin 1" Frame

Outdoor Sofa

PATINA FARM

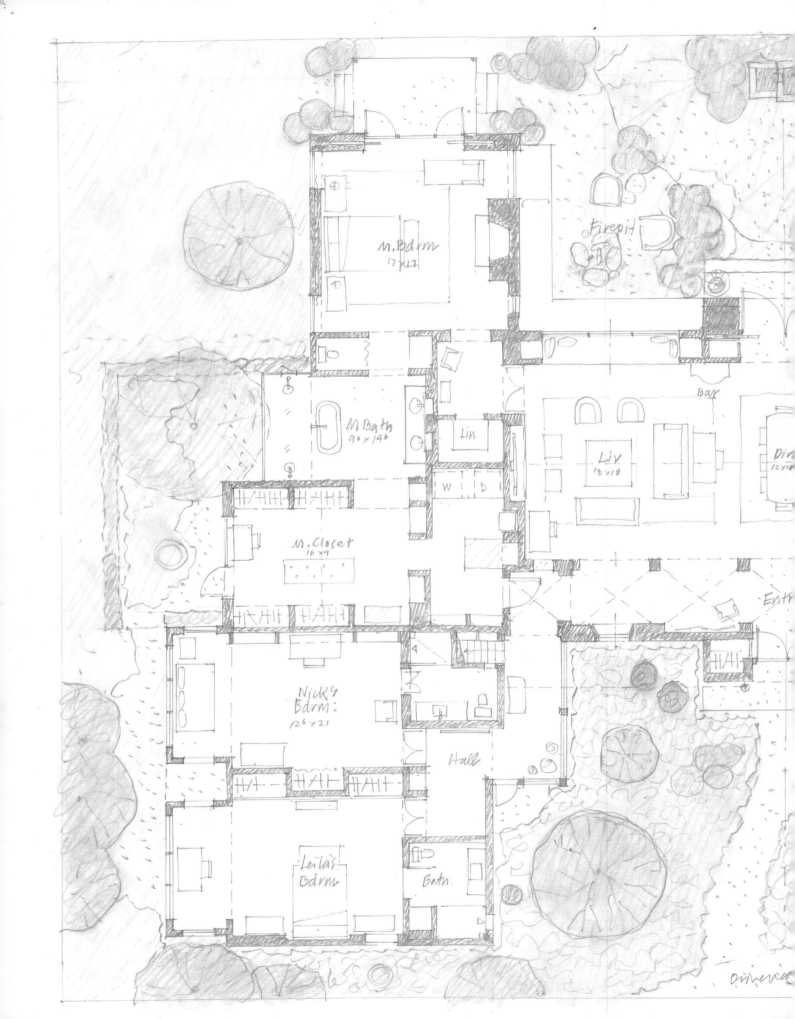

M. Bdrm
17 x 17

Firepit

Bar

M Bath
9'6 x 14'6

Lin

Liv
18 x 18

Din
12 x 18

M. Closet
16 x 9

W   D

Entr

Nick's
Bdrm:
12'6 x 21

Hall

Leila's
Bdrm

Bath.